JAVASCRIPT

MIKE McGRATH

in
easy steps

In easy steps is an imprint of Computer Step
Southfield Road . Southam
Warwickshire CV47 0FB . United Kingdom
www.ineasysteps.com

Notice of Liability
Every effort has been made to ensure that this book contains accurate and current information. However, Computer Step and the author shall not be liable for any loss or damage suffered by readers as a result of any information contained herein.

Trademarks
All trademarks are acknowledged as belonging to their respective companies.

Printed and bound in the United Kingdom

ISBN 1-84078-255-2

Contents

Introducing JavaScript

Welcome to the world of JavaScript. This chapter introduces the JavaScript language and illustrates how to add JavaScript to a HTML document. The JavaScript language keywords are all listed and the essentials of functions and variables are explained.

Covers

Chapter One

Introduction

JavaScript is an interpreted programming language whose interpreter is embedded inside Web browser software, such as Microsoft Internet Explorer and Netscape Navigator.

This means that script contained in Web documents can be read by the browser's JavaScript engine whenever the document is loaded into the browser window.

The JavaScript interpreter is an integral part of the browser software so scripts are parsed without delay.

In this way, Web documents can be made to respond to the user's actions and to perform dynamic visual effects.

JavaScript should not be confused with the compiled programming language called Java from Sun Microsystems which, although bearing some resemblance, is a completely different language.

JavaScript appeared in December 1995 and was initially called LiveScript, although the name was soon changed for marketing reasons.

The JavaScript language contains many impressive features but for security reasons it cannot read or write files, with the exception of cookie files that store a small amount of data.

This book is concerned with the core and client-side features of JavaScript that are most useful in the creation of interactive Web pages.

It is important to learn the basics – so the mechanics of the language are covered first in chapters that explain, by example, how to write JavaScript programs.

Then the browser Document Object Model (DOM) is introduced to illustrate how all Web pages contain objects with properties that can be manipulated by JavaScript.

Combining JavaScript with knowledge of the DOM allows the creation of powerful Dynamic HTML (DHTML) effects.

The final part of this book contains examples of JavaScript in use to create popular DHTML effects, together with full source code that can be used on any Web page.

Including JavaScript in HTML

In order to include JavaScript in a Web document a script block can be defined within the HTML code.

The script block may be defined anywhere within the HTML code although the usual place is inside the head section of the document, between the **<head>** and **</head>** tags.

When a browser loads a document it reads (parses) the code sequentially. So placing the script block in the head of the document ensures that the JavaScript code is parsed before the rest of the HTML code and document's body content.

A script block looks like this :

```
<script type = "text/javascript">

</script>
```

The actual code could be added between the HTML **<script>** and **</script>** tags.

Alternatively, JavaScript code may be separated from the HTML code by writing all the JavaScript code inside a JavaScript file. This is simply a text document, that is saved with a **.js** file extension, and contains no HTML tags whatsoever.

The script reference should still be placed in the document head section with an added **src** attribute pointing the browser to the URL address of the JavaScript file, like in this example:

Notice that the ***</script>*** *closing tag is still required.*

```
<script type = "text/javascript" src = "mycode.js">

</script>
```

This is a better method than writing the code in a script block within the HTML document as it makes the code easier to maintain, avoids conflicts between JavaScript and XML, and allows the JavaScript code to be accessible to several HTML documents.

All the JavaScript examples listed in this book are written in JavaScript files that are named as their HTML counterpart. For instance, **hello.html** calls upon the JavaScript code in **hello.js**.

Hello World

To make a JavaScript alert dialog box appear is just a matter of calling the intrinsic JavaScript **alert()** function, like this:

```
alert( "Hello World" );
```

hello-alert.js

This script can now be included in a HTML document by adding a **<script>** element specifying its type and URL address:

hello-alert.html (head section only)

```
<head>
  <title>Hello World</title>
  <script type= "text/javascript" src= "hello-alert.js">
  </script>
</head>
```

This same method of including JavaScript files in a HTML document is used by all the examples in this book.

When this document is loaded into the Web browser the JavaScript engine implements the instructions contained in the JavaScript code.

In this case, the JavaScript code causes the browser to open an **alert()** dialog box bearing the message contained within the quotation marks inside the brackets.

[JavaScript Application]   ✕
⚠   Hello World
OK

The title bar in the alert dialog may contain a different title – but this is not controlled by JavaScript.

The quotation marks inside the brackets do not actually appear as part of the message because they are just used by JavaScript to denote a string of characters that is the text content of the message itself.

All text strings in JavaScript are contained in this way.

Syntax rules

Notice that there is a semi-colon character at the end of the JavaScript statement on the facing page to comply with the required JavaScript language syntax rules.

This must be added at the end of every JavaScript statement – in the same way that a period is used to terminate a sentence in the English language syntax rules.

Most importantly, JavaScript is a case-sensitive language where "ALERT", "Alert" and "alert" are seen as three different words.

Problems with case can be avoided by using only lowercase throughout JavaScript code.

All JavaScript keywords are in lowercase only so using ALERT("Hello World") or Alert("Hello World") in the previous code example would not call the JavaScript **alert()** function.

Spaces, tabs and new lines are collectively known as **whitespace** and are completely ignored by JavaScript so the code may be formatted and indented to make its appearance more easily human-readable.

It is often useful to add comments to JavaScript code as explanation. The parser sees any text between **//** and the end of that line as a single-line comment, which it ignores. Also any text, on one or more lines, between **/*** and ***/** is ignored.

comments.js

```
/* Here is an introduction
to this script code that
uses a multi-line comment */

// This is a single-line comment

// Display a greeting
alert( "Hello World" );
```

Excessive commenting is best avoided – this can dramatically increase the size of a JavaScript file.

Keywords

The following table contains the keywords that are part of the JavaScript language syntax. These may not be used when choosing identifier names for variables, functions or labels:

break	do	function	null	typeof
case	else	if	return	var
continue	export	import	switch	void
default	false	in	this	while
delete	for	new	true	with

JavaScript keywords must always appear in lower case.

Additionally, JavaScript reserves all the words listed in the table below for possible future inclusion into the JavaScript syntax – so these too may not be used as identifier names. Although this may seem to be a lot of words to avoid it is seldom a real problem – it's just a point to remember.

abstract	debugger	goto	package	synchronized
boolean	double	implements	private	throw
byte	enum	instanceof	protected	throws
catch	extends	int	public	transient
char	final	interface	short	try
class	finally	long	static	
const	float	native	super	

Variables

A variable is a place in which to store data for manipulation within a JavaScript program.

When naming variables any letter, digit and the underscore character _ may be used but the variable name may not begin with a digit. These are all valid variable names:

```
abc

my_first_variable

var123
```

Create a new variable using the JavaScript **var** keyword:

first-var.js

```javascript
// create a variable and assign a string to it
var message = "My First JavaScript Variable";

// display the value stored in the variable
alert( message );
```

The text string is stored inside the variable named **message**.

The variable name is used in the call to the JavaScript **alert()** function that opens an alert dialog box displaying the string that is stored in the **message** variable.

[JavaScript Application]

⚠ My First JavaScript Variable

OK

Data types

JavaScript is a loosely typed language so its variables can store numbers, text strings or boolean values (ie. **true** or **false**).

This is unlike other programming languages such as C++ and Java that need to declare variables of a specific data type and can only then store data of the declared type.

data-types.js

```
// initialize a number variable
var a = 0.06;

// initialize a string
var b = "JavaScript in easy steps";

// initialize a boolean variable
var c = false;

// display the data type of each variable
alert( typeof a + "\n" + typeof b + "\n" + typeof c );
```

The example above creates variables with initial values of the three different data types supported by JavaScript.

Notice that JavaScript makes no distinction between integer numbers and floating-point numbers.

These three values are first passed to the **alert()** function, then the JavaScript keyword **typeof** is used to return their data types for display in the alert dialog box shown below.

The code **"+\n+"** inside the brackets just displays the output for each value on a new line in the alert dialog box.

[JavaScript Application] ⊠

⚠ number
string
boolean

[OK]

Escape sequences

When a character in a string is preceded by the \ backslash character there is a special effect on the character immediately following the backslash. This is known as an escape sequence as it allows the character to escape recognition as part of the JavaScript syntax.

The table below lists more escape sequences:

The code example on the facing page uses the \n newline escape.

\b	Backspace
\f	Form feed
\n	New line
\r	Carriage return
\'	Single quote
\"	Double quote
\\	Single backslash character

The escape sequence \" is useful to incorporate quotation marks within a string without the string itself becoming terminated, as in this example:

escapes.js

```
// display the string with escaped quotes
alert( "We all say \"JavaScript is great!\" " );
```

Functions

A function is a piece of JavaScript code that can be executed once or many times by the JavaScript application. Functions and variables form the basis of all JavaScript programming.

This is how a function looks:

first-fcn.html

```
// a function to display a message in an alert dialog
function call_alert()
{
    alert( "My First JavaScript Function" );
}
```

Always try to give meaningful names to functions and variables, describing their purpose.

Create a new function using the JavaScript **function** keyword followed by a given identifier name. The name must be unique within the script and adhere to the same naming conventions that apply to the naming of variables.

The name is always followed by a pair of plain brackets, then a pair of curly brackets containing the code to be executed.

In the example, the function has been named **call_alert()** and the code to be executed will call the JavaScript **alert()** function to display an **alert()** dialog box containing a message.

Remember to include the plain brackets when referring to a function.

The function can be called from anywhere in the JavaScript file or in the HTML document to execute the statement that it contains.

For instance, the **onload** attribute of the HTML **<body>** tag can be used to call the function when the document is loaded into the browser, like this:

```
<body onload = "call_alert()">
```

[JavaScript Application]

⚠ My First JavaScript Function

OK

Function arguments

The plain brackets that follow the name of all functions may be used to contain data for use in the code to be executed. Just as the brackets of the JavaScript **alert()** function contain the string to be displayed in the **alert()** dialog box it creates.

The data contained within the brackets is known as the function "argument".

In the example below the function call passes a text string to the argument named **str** in the **call_alert()** function for use in the code that is to be executed:

fcn-args.js

```
// a function to display the value of a passed argument
function call_alert( str )
{
  alert( str );
}
```

It is important to note that string contained inside the call to this function is enclosed in single quotes to differentiate it from the double quotes used to contain the entire call:

```
<body onload = "call_alert( 'Passed Value' )">
```

str is often used in JavaScripts as a variable name for strings.

Using double quotes for both would mean that the onload attribute value would be **"call_alert("** because the string is terminated by the second double quote. This would create a browser error and the function would not be executed.

The use of single and double quotes in this manner appears throughout JavaScript programming in several ways.

[JavaScript Application] ✕

⚠ Passed Value

OK

Multiple functions

JavaScript functions may call other functions during the execution of their code in just the same way that the previous examples called the JavaScript **alert()** function.

The following example demonstrates the use of multiple functions to manipulate and display an integer argument:

multi-fcn.js

```
// a function to call a second function
// and display a returned result
function call_alert( num )
{
  var new_number = make_double( num );
  alert( "The Value Is " + new_number );
}

// a function to double a value
// and return the result to the caller
function make_double( num )
{
  var double_num = num + num;
  return double_num;
}
```

The argument value is passed from the caller to the **make_double()** function via the **call_alert()** function:

```
<body onload = "call_alert( 4 )">
```

The plus sign is used both to concatenate text when used with strings and to perform addition when used with numbers.

The value is manipulated by the code in the function body and the result is returned to the **new_number** variable in the **call_alert()** function using the JavaScript **return** keyword. Finally the **alert()** function is called to display the **new_number** variable value.

[JavaScript Application] ✕

⚠ The Value Is 8

OK

Variable scope

The variables used in the example on the facing page are both declared inside a function so they are called **local** variables. Local variables can only be used by the function in which they are declared.

Conversely, **global** variables are declared outside functions and can be accessed by any function in the same document.

var-scope.js

```
// create a global variable
var stored_num;

// a function to call a second function
// and display a returned result
function call_alert( num )
{
  stored_num = num;
  make_triple();
  alert( "The Value Is " + stored_num );
}

// a function to double a value
// and return the result to the caller
function make_triple()
{
  stored_num = stored_num + stored_num + stored_num;
}
```

All variables may simply be declared without being initialized with a value.

This example passes the argument value to a global variable:

```
<body onload = "call_alert( 5 )">
```

The second function manipulates the value of the global variable before calling **alert()** to display the new value.

[JavaScript Application]

⚠ The Value Is 15

OK

Multiple arguments

JavaScript functions may contain multiple arguments if they are separated by a comma.

The number of arguments defined when the function is declared must be exactly matched by the number of arguments contained in any call to that function.

This example declares a function containing three arguments – so any call to it must contain three argument values:

multi-args.js

```javascript
// create three variables
var a, b, c;

// a function to display three concatenated arguments
function call_alert( str1, str2, str3 )
{
  a = str1;
  b = str2;
  c = str3;
  alert( a + b + c );
}
```

*The **var** keyword can be used to declare multiple variables by separating the variable names with a comma.*

The caller passes three strings to the function although the value of the second string is merely a space:

```html
<body onload = "call_alert('Great',' ','JavaScript')">
```

The function assigns the argument values to three global variables and then calls **alert()** to display the global values as a single concatenated string.

Performing operations

All the common JavaScript operators are detailed in this chapter which illustrates by example how to perform arithmetical operations, how to assign values and how to make comparisons. The logical operators are explained and demonstrated too, along with the conditional operator.

Covers

Chapter Two

Arithmetical operators

The arithmetical operators commonly used in JavaScript are listed in the table below with the operations they perform:

Operator	Operation
+	Addition (and concatenates strings)
-	Subtraction
*	Multiplication
/	Division
%	Modulus
++	Increment
--	Decrement

Notice that the **+** operator has two types of operation depending on the given operands. It will add together two numeric values and give the result of the addition. It will also join together two string values and return the concatenated string, as in the example on the facing page.

*An example using the modulus operator to determine odd or even values can be found in the **if** statement example on page 32.*

The **%** modulus operator will divide the first given number by the second given number and return the remainder of the operation. This is most useful to determine if a number has an odd or even value.

The **++** increment and **--** decrement operators alter the given value by 1 and return the resulting new value. These are most commonly used to count iterations in a loop.

All the other operators act as you would expect but care should be taken to bracket expressions where more than one operator is being used to clarify the operations:

```
a = b * c - d % e / f ;          \\ This is unclear

a = (b * c) - ((d % e) / f );    \\ This is clearer
```

Arithmetical examples

arithmetic.js

The increment and decrement operators may also be used following the operand. Note that in those cases they will perform the operation but only return the unoperated value.

```javascript
var addnum = 20 + 30;                          // addition

var addstr = "I love " + "JavaScript";   // concatenation

var sub = 35.75 - 28.25;                       // subtraction

var mul = 8 * 50;                              // multiplication

var mod =  65 % 2;                             // modulus

var inc = 5 ; inc = ++inc;                     // increment

var dec = 5 ; dec = --dec;                     // decrement

var result = "Addnum is " + addnum + "\n";

result += "Addstr is " + addstr + "\n";

result += "Sub is " + sub + "\n";

result += "Mul is " + mul + "\n";

result += "Mod is " + mod + "\n";

result += "Inc is " + inc + "\n";

result += "Dec is " + dec + "\n";

alert ( result );
```

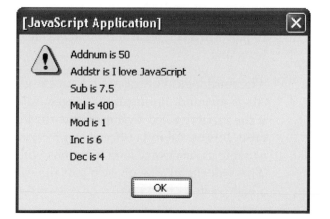

Logical operators

The three logical operators that can be used in JavaScript are listed in the table below:

Operator	Operation
&&	Logical AND
||	Logical OR
!	Logical NOT

The logical operators are used with operands that have the boolean values of **true** or **false** – or values that can convert to **true** or **false**.

The logical **&&** operator will evaluate two operands and return **true** only if both operands themselves are **true**. Otherwise the **&&** operator will return **false**.

There is an example of conditional branching in the conditional operator demo on page 30.

This is typically used in conditional branching where the direction of a JavaScript application is determined by testing two conditions. If both conditions are satisfied the script will go in a certain direction otherwise the script will take a different direction.

Unlike the **&&** operator that needs both operands to be **true** the **||** operator will evaluate its two operands and return **true** if either one of the operands itself returns **true**. If neither operand returns **true** then **||** will return **false**. This is useful in a JavaScript application to perform a certain action if either one of two test conditions has been met.

The third logical operator **!** is a unary operator that is used before a single operand. It returns the inverse value of the given operand, so if the variable **a** had a value of **true** then **!a** would have a value of **false**. It is useful in JavaScript applications to toggle the value of a variable in successive loop iterations with a statement like **a=!a**. This will ensure that on each pass the value is changed, like flicking a light switch on and off.

Logical examples

logical.js
(part of)

```
var a = true , b = false;

var test1 = ( a && a );   // test both operands for true

var test2 = ( a && b );

var test3 = ( b && b );

var test4 = ( a || b );   // test either operand for true

var test5 = ( a || b );

var test6 = ( b || b );

var test7 = !a ; var test8 = !b;    // invert values

var result = "AND \n";

result += "1: " +test1+ "    2: " +test2+ "    3: "+test3;

result += "\n\nOR\n";

result += "4: "+test4+"    5: "+test5+"    6: "+test6;

result += "\n\nNOT\n7: " +test7+ "    8: " + test8;

alert( result );
```

*Use the **\n** new line escape, and spaces to format the displayed output string.*

[JavaScript Application]

⚠ AND
    1: true 2: false 3: false

    OR
    4: true 5: true 6: false

    NOT
    7: false 8: true

OK

Assignment operators

The operators that are commonly used in JavaScript to assign values are all listed in the table below. All except the simple = assign operator are a shorthand form of a longer expression so each equivalent is also given for clarity.

Operator	Example	Equivalent
=	a = b	a = b
+=	a += b	a = (a + b)
-=	a -= b	a = (a - b)
*=	a *= b	a = (a * b)
/=	a /= b	a = (a / b)
%=	a %= b	a = (a % b)

 The equality operator compares values and is explained fully, with examples, on page 28.

It is important to think of the = operator as meaning "assign" rather than "equals" to avoid confusion with the == equality operator.

In the example in the table the variable named **a** is assigned the value that is contained in the variable named **b** to become its new value.

The **+=** operator is most useful and has been used in earlier examples to add a second string to an existing string. In the table example the **+=** operator adds the value contained in variable **a** to the value contained in the variable named **b** then assigns the result to become the new value contained in variable **a**.

All other operators in the table work in the same way – by making the arithmetical operation between the two values first, then assigning the result to the first variable to become its new value.

Assignment examples

assignment.js
(part of)

```javascript
var a= "JavaScript", b= " Code";  // assign string values

a += b;                // concatenate strings and assign to a

var c= 8, d= 4;                   // assign integer values

c += d;                // add numbers and assign result to c

var e= 7.5, f= 2.25;              // assign float values

e -= f;         // subtract f from e and assign result to e

var g= 8, h= 4;                   // assign integer values

g *= h;         // multiply numbers and assign result to g

var i= 8, j= 4;                   // assign integer values

i /= j;          // divide i by j and assign result to i

var k= 8, l= 4;                   // assign integer values

k %= l;          // divide k by l and assign remainder to k
```

*The results are displayed using the **alert()** function, as before, but that part of the code has been omitted to save space.*

[JavaScript Application]   ☒

⚠ ADD & ASSIGN STRING a: JavaScript Code

ADD & ASSIGN INTEGER c: 12

SUBTRACT & ASSIGN FLOAT e: 5.25

MULTIPLY & ASSIGN g: 32

DIVIDE & ASSIGN i: 2

MODULUS & ASSIGN k: 0

[OK]

Comparison operators

The operators that are commonly used in JavaScript to compare two values are all listed in the table below:

Operator	Comparative Test
==	Equality
!=	Inequality
>	Greater than
<	Less than
>=	Greater than or equal to
<=	Less than or equal to

An example of the < less than operator in a JavaScript loop statement can be found on page 36.

The == equality operator compares two operands and will return **true** if both are equal in value. If both are the same number they are equal, or if both are strings containing the same characters in the same positions they are equal. Boolean operands that are both **true**, or both **false**, are equal.

Conversely the != operator returns true if two operands are not equal using the same rules as the == operator.

Equality and inequality operators are useful in testing the state of two variables to perform conditional branching.

The > greater than operator compares two operands and will return **true** if the first is greater in value than the second.

The < less than operator makes the same comparison but will return **true** if the first operand is less in value than the second.

Adding the = operator after a > greater than operator or a > less than operator makes it also return **true** if the two operands are exactly equal in value.

The > greater than operator is frequently used to test the value of a countdown variable in a loop.

Comparison examples

comparison.js
(part of)

```javascript
// compare string values
var teststrings1 = ( "JavaScript" == "JavaScript" );

var teststrings2 = ( "JavaScript" == "javascript" );

// compare numeric values
var testnumbers1 = ( 1.785 == 1.785 );

var testnumbers2 = ( 5 != 5 );

// compare boolean values
var testbooleans1 = ( true == true );

var testbooleans2 = ( false != false );

var testlessthan1 = ( 100 < 200 );

var testlessthan2 = ( 100 < 100 );

var testlessthan_or_equal = ( 100 <= 100 );

var testgreaterthan = ( -1 > 1 );

var a = 8, b = 8.0, testvariables1 = ( a == b );

var c = null, d = null, testvariables2 = ( c == d );
```

Notice that the capitalization should also match to make strings equal.

null is a JavaScript keyword meaning there is no value.

The results are displayed using the alert() function, as before, but that part of the code has been omitted to save space.

[JavaScript Application]

TEST STRINGS 1: true 2: false

TEST NUMBERS 1: true 2: false

TEST BOOLEANS 1: true 2: false

TEST LESS THAN 1: true 2: false

TEST LESS THAN OR EQUAL: true

TEST GREATER THAN: false

TEST VARIABLES 1: true 2: true

OK

Conditional operator

The JavaScript coder's favorite comparison operator is probably the conditional operator. This first evaluates an expression for a **true** or **false** value then executes one of two given statements, depending on the result of the evaluation.

The conditional operator has this syntax:

```
(test expression) ? if-true-do-this : if-false-do-this ;
```

This operator can often be used to run script functions that are dedicated to a particular Web browser following a browser-identification routine. The example below is to display a welcome message determined by browser type:

conditional.js
(part of)

```
// Is the browser Internet Explorer ?
var is_ie = browser_id();

// Display appropriate greeting
( is_ie ) ? greet_ie() : greet_other();
```

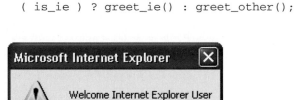

See page 92 for more on browser identification.

Making statements

Statements are used in JavaScript to progress the execution of the JavaScript application. They may define loops within the code or be simple terms to be evaluated. This chapter examines conditional testing and the different types of loops with examples of their use.

Covers

Chapter Three

Conditional if

The **if** keyword is used to perform the basic conditional JavaScript test to evaluate an expression for a boolean value. The statement following the evaluation will only be executed when the expression returns true. The syntax for the **if** statement looks like this:

```
if (test expression) statement-to-execute-when-true ;
```

The code to be executed may contain multiple statements if they are enclosed within a pair of curly braces to form a statement block.

In the example below the expression to be tested uses the modulus operator to determine if the value contained in the variable called **num** is exactly divisible by 2. The statement block has two statements – one to assign a string value to a variable and another to call a JavaScript function.

if.js

```
// create two variables
var msg, num;

num = 7;

// test if the number is not exactly divisible by 2
if ( num % 2 != 0 )
{
    msg = num + " is an odd number.";
    alert( msg );
}
```

The expression could have used (num%2==1) to detect an odd number.

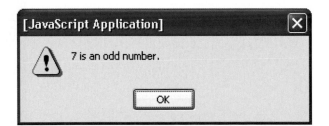

If - prompt example

This example calls the JavaScript **prompt()** function which needs two arguments to be supplied by the caller. The first argument is the message to be displayed and the second is a default entry in the input field – in this case an empty string.

The user input is assigned to the **username** variable and is displayed by the **alert()** function if the string is not still empty.

if-prompt.js

The prompt dialog will open with an empty input field but is shown here following user input.

```
// initialize a variable with a null value
var username = null;

if ( username == null )
{
  // ask the user for their name
  username = prompt( "Please Enter Your Name", "" );

  // ... or greet the user by name
  if ( username != "" ) alert( "Welcome " + username );
}
```

If - else statements

The JavaScript **else** keyword can be used with an **if** statement to provide alternative code to execute, in the event that the test expression returns **false**.

This is known as conditional branching and has this syntax:

```
if (test expression) do-this ; or-else-do-this ;
```

The semicolon is required after the first statement before starting the else alternative code.

Several expressions may be tested until a **true** value is found when the code following the true expression will be executed. It is important to note any further code contained in the **if-else** statement is ignored.

So in the following example any code after the call to the **alert()** function by the third test will be ignored completely:

if-else.js

```javascript
var num = 2, bool = false;

// is the number 1 and the boolean value true ?
if(num == 1 && bool == 1)  alert("TEST1 bool: " + bool);
else

// is the number 2 and the boolean value true ?
if(num == 2 && bool == 1)  alert("TEST2 bool: " + bool);
else

// is the number 2 and the boolean value false ?
if(num == 2 && bool == 0)  alert("TEST3 bool: " + bool);
else

// is the number 3 and the boolean value false ?
if(num == 3 && bool == 0)  alert("TEST4 bool: " + bool);
```

*Boolean values in JavaScript can also be written numerically as 1 (**true**) and 0 (**false**).*

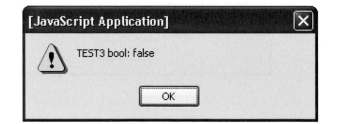

[JavaScript Application]

⚠ TEST3 bool: false

OK

The switch statement

Conditional branching using the **if-else** statement may be more efficiently performed using a **switch** statement when a test expression evaluates the value of just one variable.

The **switch** statement works in an unusual way – first it evaluates a given expression, then it seeks a label to match the resulting value. The code associated with the matching label will be executed or, if no match is made, the statement will execute any default code.

The JavaScript **case** keyword is used to denote a label and the **default** keyword denotes the default code.

*For more detail on the **break** statement see page 40.*

All label code must be terminated by a break statement using the JavaScript **break** keyword.

The labels may be numbers, strings, or booleans but must all be of the same type, like in this example that uses number types:

switch.js

```
var num = 2;

switch(num)
{
    // is the number 1 ?
    case 1 : alert("This is case 1 code"); break;

    // is the number 2 ?
    case 2 : alert("This is case 2 code"); break;

    // is the number 3 ?
    case 3 : alert("This is case 3 code"); break;

    // if none of those numbers do this...
    default : alert("This is default code");
}
```

Omitting the ending break keywords will allow execution of all other code in the switch statement.

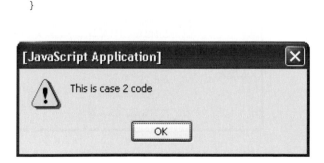

```
[JavaScript Application]                    [X]

    /!\     This is case 2 code

                    [   OK   ]
```

For loops

The **for** loop is probably the most frequently used type of loop in JavaScript and has this syntax:

> **for (** *initializer* **, ** *test* **, ** *increment* **) ** *statement/s* **;**

The initializer is used to set the start value for the counter of the number of loop iterations. A variable may be declared here for this purpose and it is traditional to name it **i**.

At each pass of the loop a boolean condition is tested and the next iteration of the loop will only run if the condition returns **true**. If the test returns **false** then the loop will end.

With every iteration the counter is incremented then the loop will execute the code in the statement. Multiple statements can be executed if they are contained by curly braces in a statement block.

The following example makes five iterations and changes the assigned value of two variables at each pass:

for.js

```
var a = 0, b = 0;

// initialize counter at zero then loop until it hits 5
for ( var i = 0; i < 5; i++ )
{
   // increment variable values on each iteration
   a += 10; b += 5;
}

// display the final values after the loop ends...
alert( "FOR LOOP\n\n A is " + a + "... B is " + b );
```

*A **for** loop can also count down – decrementing the counter at each iteration.*

[JavaScript Application] ✕

⚠ FOR LOOP

A is 50... B is 25

OK

The for - in loop

The **for-in** loop has a special use to enumerate all the variables or properties contained within an object.

This loop is seldom used in regular JavaScript but is included here because it can reveal the properties available for manipulation within a Web browser.

The following example reveals a tantalizing glimpse of the properties available within the window object of the Microsoft Internet Explorer 6.0 Web browser:

for-in.js

```
var i = 0 ; a = "";

// list all window properties in a variable
for ( property in window )
{
  a += property + "...";
}

// display the window properties list
alert( a );
```

The properties revealed will vary for each browser and version.

The properties revealed with this script are part of the Document Object Model (DOM) that is described in chapter 8.

Microsoft Internet Explorer

⚠ onbeforeunload...onafterprint...
top...location...
parent...offscreenBuffering...
frameElement...onerror...
screen...event...
clipboardData...onresize...
defaultStatus...onblur...
window...onload...
onscroll...screenTop...
onfocus...Option...
length...onbeforeprint...
frames...self...
clientInformation...external...
screenLeft...opener...
onunload...document...
closed...history...
Image...navigator...
status...onhelp...
name...

[OK]

While loops

Another loop uses the JavaScript **while** keyword followed by an expression to be evaluated for a boolean value.

If the evaluation returns **true** then the code in the statement block will be executed. After the code has executed the test expression will again be evaluated and the loop will continue until the evaluation returns **false**.

An infinite loop will lock the script and crash the browser.

The statement block must feature code that will affect the test expression in order to change the evaluation result to return **false** – otherwise an infinite loop will be created.

It is important to note that if the test expression returns **false** when it is first evaluated then the code in the statement block is never executed.

This example decrements a variable value on each iteration of the loop. The counter increments until it reaches 10 when the evaluation returns **false** and the loop ends.

while.js

```
var i = 0, num = 50;

// loop until the counter hits 10
while( i < 10 )
{
  num--;
  i++;
}

// display the final counter and number values
alert( "Loop stopped at " + i + "\nnum is now " + num );
```

[JavaScript Application]

⚠ Loop stopped at 10
num is now 40

OK

The do - while loop

The JavaScript **do** keyword is used to denote the start of a **do-while** loop and is followed by a statement block containing the code to be executed by the loop.

The statement code is followed by the JavaScript **while** keyword and an expression to be evaluated for a boolean value of **true** or **false**.

If the evaluation returns **true** the loop restarts at the **do** keyword and will continue until the evaluation returns **false**.

It is important to note that, unlike the simple **while** loop, the statement code will always be executed at least once by the **do-while** loop because the test expression is not encountered until the end of the loop.

The following example will never loop because the counter value is incremented to 1 in the first execution of the statement code so the first test evaluation will return **false**:

do-while.js

```
var i = 0, num = 50;

// loop until the counter hits 1
do
{
  num--;
  i++;
} while( i < 1 );

// display the final counter and number values
alert("Loop stopped at " + i + "\nnum is now " + num );
```

*A **while** loop is often more suitable than a **do-while** loop.*

[JavaScript Application]

⚠ Loop stopped at 1
num is now 49

[OK]

Break statement

The JavaScript **break** keyword is used to terminate the execution of a loop prematurely.

The **break** keyword is situated inside the statement block containing the code that the loop should execute and is preceded by a conditional test.

When the test condition is met the **break** statement immediately terminates the loop and no further iterations are made.

Notice in the **alert()** output below that the counter value is still three because the increment in the final iteration is not applied

In the following example the conditional test will return **true** when the counter value reaches three:

break.js

The **break** keyword is also used as a terminator with a **switch** statement.

```
var i= 0;

// loop until the counter hits 6
while( i < 6 )
{
  if( i == 3 ) break;
  i++;
}

// display the final counter value
alert("BREAK\n\nLoop stopped at " + i );
```

[JavaScript Application]

⚠ BREAK

Loop stopped at 3

OK

Continue statement

The JavaScript **continue** keyword is used to break the current iteration of a loop.

Just like the **break** keyword the **continue** keyword is situated inside the statement block containing the code that the loop should execute, preceded by a conditional test.

When the test condition is met the **continue** keyword immediately stops the current iteration of the loop, but further iterations will be made until the loop ends.

In the example below the test condition is met when the counter value reaches three so the string concatenation in that iteration is not applied but the loop continues on:

continue.js

The loop counter should be incremented before the **continue** *condition is tested to avoid creating an infinite loop.*

```javascript
var i = 0, str = "";

// loop until the counter hits 5
while( i < 5 )
{
  i++;
  if( i == 3 )continue;
  str += i + " ";
}

// display final counter value and all series numbers
alert("CONTINUE\n\nLoop stopped:"+i+"\n\nSeries:"+str );
```

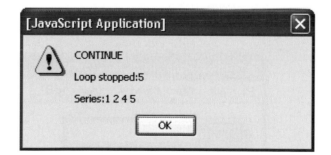

Using with statements

The JavaScript **with** keyword is used to reference object properties without needing to add the object name before each property name.

See Chapter 10 for more about document objects and properties.

This is most useful when writing JavaScript applications to produce dynamic effects as these scripts often refer to document objects.

For example, every Web page contains a **document** object that in turn has a **forms** property to reference forms on the Web page. Forms can be referenced by the value assigned to their **id** attribute. Individual form fields can be referenced by the value assigned to their **name** attribute and JavaScript can set their values.

*The **<script>** element that includes the JavaScript file must appear after the form in the HTML file – so that the form fields are created before the script tries to set their values.*

In this example the script sets **user** and **city** fields of an **order** form:

```
document.forms.order.user.value = "Mike";

document.forms.order.city.value = "New York";
```

These assignments can be expressed more clearly using a **with** statement like this:

with.js

```
// set values for user and city fields of the order form
with( document.forms.order )
{
  user.value = "Mike";
  city.value = "New York";
}
```

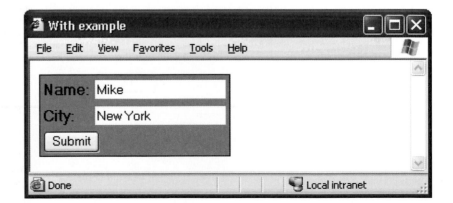

Using arrays

This chapter deals exclusively with the topic of arrays and illustrates by example what they are and how to use them. The examples include a practical use of arrays to preload images into a Web browser.

Covers

Chapter Four

Creating arrays

An array is like a variable that can contain multiple values – unlike a regular variable that may only contain a single value.

A variable is given array status using the JavaScript **new** keyword along with the JavaScript **Array()** constructor function.

Multiple data values can then be assigned to the array using the array name together with an index number, starting at zero, placed inside square brackets, like in this example:

```javascript
// create a new array
var a = new Array();

// assign values to the first three array elements
a[0] = "First";
a[1] = "JavaScript";
a[2] = "Array";
```

Remember that an array index starts at zero. So a[2] is the third element in the index, not the second.

The array values can now be used just like regular variables.

For small arrays it is often more convenient to initialize the array values as arguments in the **Array()** constructor. This is illustrated in the example below which creates three arrays:

array.js

```javascript
// create and initialize three new arrays
var a = new Array("Jan ", "Feb ", "Mar ");
var b = new Array("21,", "22,", "23,");
var c = new Array(" 2003", " 2004", " 2005");

// concatenate and display an element from each array
alert( a[0] + b[1] + c[2] );
```

```
[JavaScript Application]                    [X]

   /!\    Jan 22, 2005

              [    OK    ]
```

Array elements

Find more on properties, objects and constructors on pages 88/89.

Each value held in an array is called an array **element**.

When a variable is given array status using the **new Array()** constructor it also gets properties and methods that can be used to manipulate the elements contained in the array.

One of the most useful of these is the **length** property that may be used to report the number of elements that the array currently contains.

The syntax to use a property or method just tacks a period and the name onto the object. So **array.length** references the **length** property of the **array** object.

Notice that an array containing three values will have a length of 3, but because indexing starts at zero the last element in the array will have an index number of only 2.

The example below demonstrates this point:

elements.js

```javascript
// create a new array
var a = new Array();
a[0] = "JAVASCRIPT ";
a[1] = "ARRAY ";
a[2] = "LENGTH";

// get the array length
var arraysize = a.length;

// display each array element and the array length
alert(a[0]+a[1]+a[2]+"\nNo.of elements is "+arraysize);
```

*Optionally the **Array()** constructor may take an argument to specify the number of array elements to create, such as:*
var a = new Array(8);

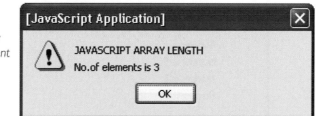

Fill elements loop

All types of loops can be used to easily fill the elements of an array with a large number of data values. This is one of the major attractions of arrays and it is achieved with very little code.

The example below first creates an array then, on each iteration, the **for** loop fills each of the array elements with a string value to which is added the current counter value.

Each element value is concatenated in the variable named **str** before finally displaying in the **alert()** dialog box:

fill.js

```
var str = "FILL ELEMENTS LOOP\n\n";

// create a new array
var arr = new Array();

// fill eight array elements
for( var i = 0; i < 8; i++ )
{
    arr[ i ] = "Number is " + i + "\n";
    str += arr[ i ];
}

// display the value stored in each array element
alert( str );
```

This code could just as easily be used to fill 100 elements by making the conditional value of 8 into 100.

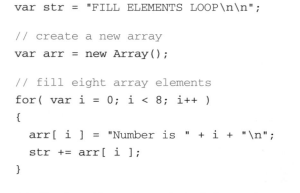

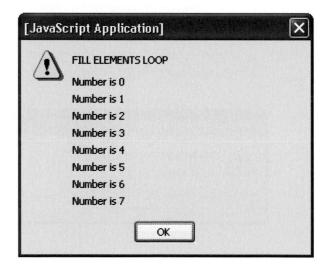

[JavaScript Application]

FILL ELEMENTS LOOP

Number is 0
Number is 1
Number is 2
Number is 3
Number is 4
Number is 5
Number is 6
Number is 7

OK

Adding more elements

Additional elements can be added to an array, without specifying an actual index number, by using the **array.length** property to find the next available empty element.

Because the **array.length** value exceeds the last index number by one it will always specify the next free element when it is used as the index number – between the square brackets.

The example below illustrates this when assigning the integer 4 to the next free element in the array named **a**.

The **b** array elements are initialized, then the **for** loop successively assigns the **b** array element values to each free element in the **a** array.

Finally all **a** array elements are displayed by the **alert()** function in concatenated form by the **array.concat()** method.

more.js

```
var a = new Array( 1, 2, 3 );

// insert an integer into the next empty element
a[ a.length ] = 4;               // a.length is 3

var b = new Array( 5, 6, 7 );

// copy each b element value into the empty a elements
for(var i = 0; i < b.length; i++ )
{
   a[a.length] = b[i];
}

// display all a element values
alert( a.concat() );
```

> **HOT TIP**
>
> The method *array.concat()* will display all the element values in an array, separated by commas.

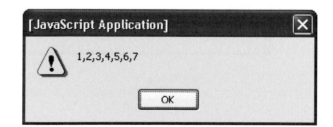

String of elements

The JavaScript **array.join()** method will convert all array elements to strings and concatenate them.

Used without arguments this will return a list of all the array element values separated by commas, like the **array.concat()** method on the previous page.

But the **array.join()** method can accept an optional argument to specify an alternative separator to the default comma separator.

Most usefully this can be a space so that result of the **array.join()** method will be a single string with space separators, as illustrated in the example below:

join.js

Escape the single quotes with a \ backslash to avoid errors.

```javascript
// create a new array
var a = new Array();

// put a word in seven array elements
a[0] = "It";
a[1] = "isn\'t";
a[2] = "rocket";
a[3] = "science -";
a[4] = "it\'s";
a[5] = "just";
a[6] = "JavaScript";

// display all words in the array, separated by a space
alert( a.join(" ") );
```

Reverse element order

Arrays can be used to contain a file name or complete URL address in each element for use with dynamic features in Web pages.

One such popular use is with JavaScript slide shows that rotate a series of images with a specified interval between each one.

A complete slide show script is given on page 166.

An array is used to hold the URL of each image in its elements so that the script can easily reference them by array index.

If the slide show is required to reverse after displaying the final image, rather than start over at the first image, this can be achieved by reversing the element order inside the array.

The following example creates an initial array of just three images whose order will be reversed after the final image displays and the **rev** variable is set to **true**:

reverse.js

```
// create a new array of image URLs
var imgs = new Array("img1.gif","img2.gif","img3.gif");

// create a control variable
var rev = false;

// when the slideshow displays the final image
// ...reverse the order
rev = true;

if( rev == true )
{
   imgs.reverse();
}

// display the reversed element order
alert( imgs.join(" - ") );
```

The evaluation (rev == true) can be abbreviated to a simple (rev).

[JavaScript Application] ⊠

⚠ img3.gif - img2.gif - img1.gif

OK

Sub-arrays

The JavaScript **array.slice()** method is useful to make a new array from an existing array using some of the existing element values.

This method takes two arguments to specify the index numbers of elements in the original array where the new array elements should start and end.

The second argument may have a negative value to indicate the element position from the end of the array.

If only a single argument is specified it will be used as the first element index number and the method will return a new array with all elements from this position onwards.

These examples illustrate the different ways in which the **array.slice()** method can be used:

slice.js

The array elements are taken up to, but not including, the second argument index.

```javascript
// create and initialize a new array
var nums = new Array( 1, 2, 3, 4, 5, 6, 7, 8 );

// get elements #2 up to #4
var str = "Slice A: " + nums.slice( 2, 4 ) + "\n";

// get elements #1 to one before the final element
str += "Slice B: " + nums.slice( 1, -1 ) + "\n";

// get elements #3 to end
str += "Slice C: " + nums.slice( 3 ) + "\n";

// display all three slices
alert(str);
```

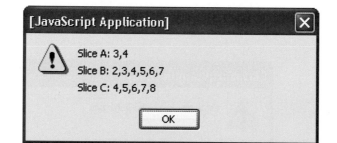

[JavaScript Application]

    Slice A: 3,4
    Slice B: 2,3,4,5,6,7
    Slice C: 4,5,6,7,8

            OK

Arrange elements

The JavaScript **array.sort()** method allows string element values to be arranged in alphabetic order.

This is sometimes desirable so that the output can be presented alphabetically.

Integer and floating point numeric values will be arranged in ascending order – as seen in the following example:

sort.js

```javascript
// create an array of integers
var integers = new Array( 3, 8, 1, 9, 7, 5, 4, 2, 6 );

// sort the integer array numerically
integers.sort();

// create an array of floating-point numbers
var floats = new Array( 0.5, 0.125, 0.75, 0.25 );

// sort the floats array numerically
floats.sort();

// create an array of strings
var strings = new Array( "Michael", "Andrew", "David" );

// sort the strings array alphabetically
strings.sort();

// separate the elements with a hyphen
var str = "Integers array: " + integers.join(" - ");
str += "\nFloats array: " + floats.join(" - ");
str += "\nStrings array: " + strings.join(" - ");

// display all three sorted arrays
alert( str );
```

Negative numeric values are arranged as -1,-2,-3, etc.

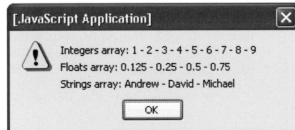

Preloader array

Rollover images in Web pages use a JavaScript effect to swap the original image for a replacement when the user places the cursor over the image.

In order for this effect to work smoothly, without any download delay, the required replacement image must be already loaded into the browser cache.

One way to do this is to use a JavaScript preload routine that forces the browser to download the image by creating **new Image()** objects that use the swap images as their source.

preload.js

```
// create an array of the URLs of all images that are to
// appear in the slideshow
var pics = new Array("pic1.gif","pic2.gif","pic3.gif");

// create a new empty array
var preload = new Array();

// insert a new Image object into each empty element
// then assign each image URL to the Image objects
for(var i = 0; i < pics.length; i++ )
{
  preload[ i ] = new Image();
  preload[ i ].src = pics[ i ];
}
```

A preload array is used with the slide show script example on page 166.

The script example above uses arrays to preload three swap images to be ready when the rollover effect is activated.

The first array contains the URL of each image file.

For each element in the **pics** array the **for** loop creates a corresponding element in the **preload** array.

Each of the **preload** elements is assigned a new **Image()** object, then the image URLs are assigned to their **src** property. This forces the browser to download each image file into its cache – ready to be displayed without delay.

Date and time

This chapter describes by example how to use date and time information in JavaScript. The Date object and the Universal Time clock are explained along with the JavaScript timer routine. There is also a full script example of a JavaScript clock.

Covers

Chapter Five

Getting date and time

Date and time is often used in JavaScript to customize the performance of a Web page. For example, a script might welcome a user with a greeting appropriate to current time:

The script for this application is contained in the example on page 56.

[JavaScript Application] ☒

⚠ Good Afternoon
Welcome to the Acme website

[OK]

The date and time that is used in JavaScript is taken from the clock and calendar in the host system that is running the browser application in which the script is loaded.

To access the system clock information the script must first create a **Date** object.

This is achieved in the same manner in which an **Array** object is created, using the JavaScript **new** keyword, but now with the JavaScript **Date()** constructor function. The example below creates and displays a new **Date** object:

date-object.js

```
// create a new Date object
var now = new Date();

// display the Date object's date and time information
alert( now );
```

[JavaScript Application] ☒

⚠ Thu Mar 31 2005 16:31:06 GMT+0100 (GMT Daylight Time)

[OK]

Date information

The **Date** object has special methods that may be used to retrieve individual parts of the date information.

Some methods return the date information as an index number that often needs to be converted by the script.

The **Date.getDay()** method returns the day of the week as an index value from 0 (Sunday) through to 6 (Saturday).

Month indexing starts at zero, not one – so the index number for March is 2 not 3.

Also the **Date.getMonth()** method returns the month of the year as an index value from 0 (January) to 11 (December).

The example below illustrates the **Date** object methods and uses two arrays to display the correct day and month names:

date.js

```
// create an array of day names
var days = new Array("Sun", "Mon", "Tue", "Wed", "Thu",
"Fri", "Sat");

// create an array of month names
var months = new Array("Jan", "Feb", "Mar", "Apr",
"May", "Jun", "Jul", "Aug", "Sep", "Oct", "Nov", "Dec");

var now = new Date();          // create a new Date object
var yy = now.getYear();                       // get the year
if(yy < 2000) yy += 1900;      // adjust year for Netscape
var mm = now.getMonth();              // get the month number
mm = months[mm];        // convert month number to name
var dd = now.getDate();      // get day number in the month
var dy = now.getDay();        // get day number in the week
dy = days[dy];               // convert day number to name

// display the extracted day and date information
alert( dy +" "+ mm +" "+ dd +" "+ yy );
```

Netscape reports the year as the number of years elapsed since 1900 – so in this case a line of script adds 1900 to the reported date.

```
[JavaScript Application]                    [X]

    /!\    Thu Mar 31 2005

                  [   OK   ]
```

Time information

The **Date** object has special methods to access the time information that it contains. The example below gets the current hours, minutes, seconds and milliseconds from the host clock and displays a welcome message appropriate for the time of day:

time.js

```
// create a new Date object
var now = new Date();

// extract the time information
var hh = now.getHours();
var mn = now.getMinutes();
var ss = now.getSeconds();
var ms = now.getMilliseconds();

// default welcome message
var hi = "Good Morning";

// welcome message if after noon
if( hh > 11 ) hi= "Good Afternoon";

// welcome message if after 6 p.m.
if( hh > 17 ) hi= "Good Evening";

// display welcome message and the current time
var tim = hi + "\n";
tim += "Hours: " +hh+ "\n";
tim += "Minutes: " +mn+ "\n";
tim += "Seconds: " +ss+ "." +ms;
alert(tim);
```

The hours are returned as numbers 0–23 in 24-hour format.

[JavaScript Application]

> Good Afternoon
> Hours: 17
> Minutes: 39
> Seconds: 16.53

[OK]

Current time

The JavaScript **Date.getTime()** method can be used to compare two date objects numerically.

The method returns a number that is the difference in milliseconds between the date object value and midnight on January 1, 1970 (sometimes referred to as "the epoch").

The example below creates a **Date** object both before and after running a loop, then compares the values returned by the **Date.getTime()** method to calculate the actual time taken to execute the loop:

elapsed-time.js

```
// create a new Date object then get the current time
var start = new Date();
var msec1 = start.getTime();

// run a loop counting up to 250,000
var num = 0;
for( var i = 0; i < 250000; i++ )
{
   num++;
}

// get another Date object and get the time now
var stop  = new Date();
var msec2 = stop.getTime();

// subtract the start time from the stop time to
// discover the amount of time between the two points
var diff = ( msec2 - msec1 ) / 1000;

// display the elapsed time
alert("Time elapsed: " +diff+ " seconds");
```

Adjust the number that the loop counts up to according to your browser and platform.

[JavaScript Application]

⚠ Time elapsed: 0.651 seconds

OK

Universal time clock

Universal Time is the standard world time clock that runs at Greenwich Mean Time.

The **Date** object methods used in the previous examples all return the local system time but sometimes it is preferable to use the standard of Universal Time.

For this the **Date** object has a series of methods that convert the time and date information from local time to universal.

The example below calls local and universal time information on a PC running at Western European Time:

utc.js

```javascript
// create a new Date object
var now = new Date();

// get the local time in hours
var hh = now.getHours();

// get the universal time in hours
var utc_hh = now.getUTCHours();

// get minutes and seconds
var mn = now.getMinutes();
var ss = now.getSeconds();

// ensure there are two digits for the minute value
if( mn <= 9 ) mn = "0" +mn;

// display both times
var wet = "Athens time: "+hh+": "+mn+": "+ss+"\n\n";
var utc = "Universal time: "+utc_hh+": "+mn+": "+ss;
alert( wet + utc );
```

If the minutes value is less than 10 this script adds a leading zero to it.

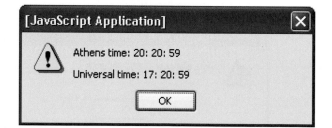

Time zones

JavaScript can determine which time zone the user is in using the **Date.getTimezoneOffset()** method.

The method gets the local time from the **Date** object then compares it to the UTC time. The return value is the difference stated in minutes because some countries have time zones at other than regular one-hour intervals.

In the example below the **Date.getTimezoneOffset()** method decides in which U.S. time zone, if any, the user is located:

time-zone.js

```
// create a new Date object
var now = new Date();

// get the number of minutes offset from UTC
var offset = now.getTimezoneOffset();

// create an empty variable
var msg;

// assign an appropriate message
switch(offset)
{
  case 240 : msg = "East Coast"; break;
  case 300 : msg = "Central"; break;
  case 360 : msg = "Mountain"; break;
  case 420 : msg = "Pacific"; break;
  default  : msg = "all";
}

// display the message
alert("Welcome to " +msg+ " visitors.");
```

This method can easily be used to redirect users to a local Web page too.

A bug in some Netscape browsers does not report the correct offset.

[JavaScript Application]   [X]

⚠ Welcome to East Coast visitors.

[OK]

Setting date and time

The JavaScript code may manipulate the **Date** object information using a variety of **Date.set()** methods.

These mirror the range of **Date.get()** methods that are used to extract parts of the **Date** object information but are used instead to set new values.

In the example below the initial **Date** object values are stored in the orig variable named **orig**. Then the various **Date.set()** methods apply new values to the **Date** object information:

set-time.js

```
// create a new Date object
var now = new Date();

// store the original date and time information
var orig = "Original :\n " +now.toString()+ "\n\n";

// set new date and time details
now.setDate(21);
now.setMonth(1);
now.setHours(12);
now.setMinutes(30);
now.setSeconds(15);
now.setFullYear(2005);

// store the modified date and time information
var mod = "Modified :\n " + now;

// display original and modified date and times
alert( orig + mod );
```

*The **toString()** method used here returns the string value of JavaScript objects and has many uses.*

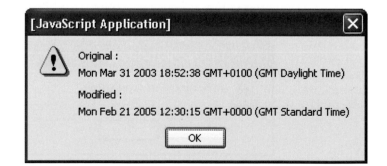

[JavaScript Application]

⚠ Original :
Mon Mar 31 2003 18:52:38 GMT+0100 (GMT Daylight Time)

Modified :
Mon Feb 21 2005 12:30:15 GMT+0000 (GMT Standard Time)

OK

Date strings

In many instances the **Date** object information must be converted into a string in order to store or use that information.

The **Date.toString()** method on the facing page does this but it is often preferable to store this information in standard UTC time.

A complete example setting cookies using this method can be found in Chapter 10, on page 114.

JavaScript provides the **Date.toGMTString()** method that both converts the information to a string and converts it to the GMT time zone.

Using this method of storing date information avoids time zone confusion and is commonly used as the standard when setting the life span of cookie files.

This simple example illustrates the **Date.toGMTString()** method performing its conversions in a browser in Tokyo, Japan:

gmt.js

```javascript
// create a new Date object
var now = new Date();

// store local time
var jpn = "Tokyo Time:\n" +now.toString()+ "\n\n";

// store GMT time
var gmt = "UTC Time:\n" + now.toGMTString();

// display local time and GMT time
alert(jpn + gmt);
```

[JavaScript Application]

Tokyo Time:
Sun Jul 13 2003 21:42:26 GMT+0900

UTC Time:
Sun, 13 Jul 2003 12:42:26 GMT

OK

Using the system clock

When a JavaScript is needed to create an action repeatedly in a Web browser window the system clock can be used with the JavaScript **setTimeout()** method of the **window** object.

The **window.setTimeout()** method can run a function after a specified interval. Two arguments are required stating the name of the function to call and the required interval time in milliseconds. This method is often used at the end of a function to call the same function recursively, following a set delay.

There is a slideshow script on page 166 using this method.

Many uses can be found for this method in creating dynamic effects. For instance, in slideshow scripts where the function displays successive images at given intervals.

The example here uses the **window.setTimeout()** method to display an **alert()** dialog box at 10 second intervals:

timeout.js

```javascript
// create and initialize a counter variable
var num = 0;

// a recursive function to display a message
function timeout()
{
  // increment the counter
  num++;
  // display the message
  alert("This is 10-Second Message No: " +num );
  // set the interval before calling this function again
  window.setTimeout("timeout()", 10000);
}

// call the function to start the routine
timeout();
```

Cancelling the timer

The unfortunate viewer of the site containing the JavaScript on the previous page would doubtless feel aggrieved at the constant alert box messages. It may be better to show the message only a couple of times then stop calling the **timeout()** function.

The **window.setTimeout()** method can be cancelled easily using the **window.clearTimeout()** method.

In order to clear the timer correctly it is necessary to assign the original **window.setTimeout()** call to a variable – so that variable can be passed as the **window.clearTimeout()** call argument.

The following example displays a message twice, then displays a final message when the timer is cleared:

two-times.js

```javascript
// create a counter variable and a timer variable
var num = 0, tim;

function timeout()
{
  num++;
  if( num == 3 )
  {
    alert("OK - I told you twice");
    window.clearTimeout( tim );    // cancel the timer
  }
  else
  {
    alert("This is 10-Second Message No : " + num );
    tim = window.setTimeout( "timeout()" , 10000); }
}

timeout();
```

*The variable name **tim** is often used to name the timer variable.*

JavaScript clock

Utilizing the **Date** object along with a timer can create a time display that updates every second to produce a clock.

The example below displays the local time dynamically in a HTML form text input named **clock** – the form **id** is simply named **f** :

clock.js

*The clock needs to be started by calling the **tick()** function from the **onload** attribute of the HTML **<body>** tag – **<body onload="tick()">**. This ensures that the form has been created before JavaScript attempts to assign the time to its **clock** form field.*

```javascript
function tick()
{
  // create a new Date object
  var now = new Date();

  // extract the current hours, minutes and seconds
  var hh = now.getHours();
  var mn = now.getMinutes();
  var ss = now.getSeconds();

  // ensure each component has two digits
  if( hh <= 9 ) hh = "0" + hh;
  if( mn <= 9 ) mn = "0" + mn;
  if(ss <= 9 ) ss = "0" + ss;

  // assign the current time string to the form field
  document.forms.f.clock.value = hh+ ": " +mn+ ": " +ss;

  // set the interval to one second
  window.setTimeout( "tick()", 1000 );
}
```

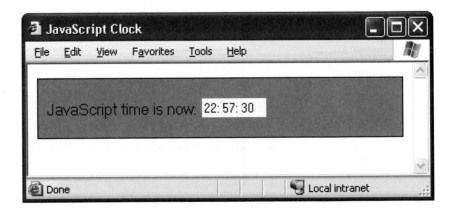

Doing mathematics

This chapter is devoted to the JavaScript **Math** object and describes the constant values and methods that are available to perform mathematical calculations. The subject of random number generation is covered and is illustrated with a practical example using random values.

Covers

Math constants

The intrinsic JavaScript **Math** object contains a number of standard mathematical constant values for easy reference.

Uppercase is always used to refer to the constant values which are all listed in the following table:

Observe correct capitalization when using any of the Math constants.

Math.E	The constant e base of the natural logarithm with a value of approximately 2.71828
Math.LN2	The natural logarithm of 2 approximately 0.69314718055994528623
Math.LN10	The natural logarithm of 10 approximately 2.3025850929940459011
Math.LOG2E	The base-2 logarithm of e approximately 1.442695040888963387
Math.LOG10E	The base-10 logarithm of e approximately 0.43429448190325181677
Math.PI	The constant pi approximately 3.14159265358979
Math.SQRT1_2	The reciprocal of the square root of 2 approximately 0.7071067811865476
Math.SQRT2	The square root of 2 with a value of approximately 1.414213562373095

The **Math** constants can be used anywhere within a script.

Most of the **Math** constants are used only in JavaScript applications that have a particular mathematical purpose but the full list is given above for completeness.

The **Math.PI** constant creates interesting possibilities with dynamic effects. The following example script dynamically rotates a layer named **dl**:

Using pi

spin.js

```javascript
// global variable to store position
var pos = 0;

// function to rotate a div with id of "d1"
function spin()
{

  // get the div's style object
  var obj_style = document.getElementById("d1").style;
  // store desired radius and x,y offsets
  var radius = 40;
  var x_offset = 50;
  var y_offset = 50;
  // increment to the new position
  pos += 10;
  // use Math to calculate the new x,y coordinates
  x = radius * Math.cos( pos * Math.PI/180 );
  y = radius * Math.sin( pos * Math.PI/180 );
  // add the x,y offsets
  x += x_offset;
  y += y_offset;
  // move the div to its new coordinates
  obj_style.left = x + "px";
  obj_style.top = y + "px";
  // set the interval to call this function again
  setTimeout( "spin()",100 );

}
```

The ***Math.cos()*** and ***Math.sin()*** methods used in this example are just some of the Math object methods detailed on the next page.

This routine is started by calling the ***spin()*** function from the ***onload*** attribute of the HTML **<body>** tag – **<body onload="spin()">**.

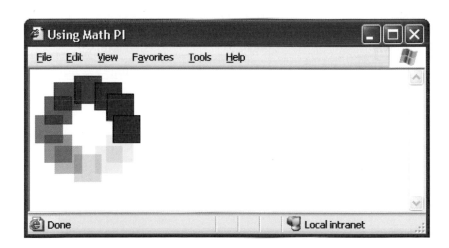

Math methods

The JavaScript **Math** object has many methods – all of them are listed in the table below:

Math.abs()	return an absolute value
Math.acos()	return an arc cosine
Math.asin()	return an arc sine
Math.atan()	return an arc tangent
Math.atan2()	return angle from an X-axis to a point
Math.ceil()	round a number up
Math.cos()	return a cosine value
Math.exp()	return an exponent of constant e
Math.floor()	round a number down
Math.log()	return a natural logarithm
Math.max()	return the larger of two numbers
Math.min()	return the smaller of two numbers
Math.pow()	return the power value
Math.random()	return a random number
Math.round()	round to the nearest integer
Math.sin()	return a sine value
Math.sqrt()	return the square root
Math.tan()	return a tangent value

HOT TIP

Math.random() has many uses in Web pages to provide varied page content.

The **Math** methods most commonly used from the above list are examined in more detail on the following pages.

Rounding floats

The **Math.round()** method in JavaScript is useful both to round floating-point numbers to the nearest integer and commute long floating-point numbers to shorter rounded versions. Commonly this will be to reduce a long floating point number to two decimal places.

If the floating point value given as the method argument is exactly halfway between two integers the method will round up to the nearest integer.

The example given below illustrates the way that the **Math.round()** method handles rounding of positive and negative halfway values and shows how it may be used to commute a long floating-point number to just two places:

round.js

```
var a = 7.5;
a = Math.round(a);
a = "Rounded Positive : "+a+ "\n";

var b = -7.5;
b = Math.round(b);
b = "Rounded Negative : "+b+ "\n";

var c = 3.764638467915;
c = c * 100;              // take it up two places
c = Math.round(c);        // do the round
c /= 100;                 // take it back down 2 places
c = "Commuted Long Float : "+c;
alert( a+b+c );
```

*Rounding **7.5** does not give the result **-8.0** because that would be a higher negative number, and so that would be rounding down*

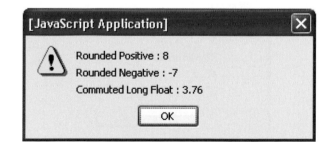

[JavaScript Application]

Rounded Positive : 8
Rounded Negative : -7
Commuted Long Float : 3.76

OK

Forcing floats

As an alternative to using the **Math.round()** method detailed on the previous page the script may require that the float be selectively forced to the nearest integer, above or below.

JavaScript provides the **Math.ceil()** method to force rounding up to the nearest integer and the **Math.floor()** method rounds to the nearest integer down.

The example below illustrates both methods in action with both positive and negative values:

ceil-floor.js

Rounding up of negative values returns the next nearest integer towards zero.

```
var a = 7.5;

var a1 = "a1 : " + Math.ceil(a);

var a2 = "a2 : " + Math.floor(a);

var b = -7.5;

var b1 = "b1 : " + Math.ceil(b);

var b2 = "b2 : " + Math.floor(b);

var rup = "ROUNDING UP\n" +a1+ "\n" +b1+ "\n\n";

var rdn = "ROUNDING DOWN\n" +a2+ "\n" +b2;

alert( rup + rdn );
```

[JavaScript Application] ✕

⚠ ROUNDING UP
a1 : 8
b1 : -7

ROUNDING DOWN
a2 : 7
b2 : -8

OK

Comparing numbers

The **Math** object has two methods allowing comparison of two numbers with a return of the higher or lower value.

Math.max() accepts the two values for comparison as arguments and will return the higher of the two values.

The **Math.min()** method works in precisely the same way but returns the lower of the two given values.

In the example below the **Math.pow()** method is used to create square and cube values that are then compared with **Math.max()** and **Math.min()**.

The **Math.pow()** method requires two arguments to specify the number then the power by which to raise that number:

maxmin-pow.js

```
var sq = Math.pow( 5, 2 );

var cb = Math.pow( 3, 3 )

var hi = "Round up : " + Math.max( sq, cb );

var lo = "Round Down : " + Math.min( sq, cb );

var ng = "Round Negative Up : " + Math.max( -5, -4.75 );

alert("MAXMIN\n\n" + hi + "\n" + lo + "\n" + ng);
```

The higher of two negative numbers is the one closest to zero.

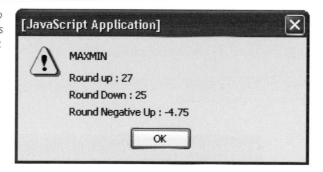

Random generator

Random numbers can be generated using the **Math.random()** method to return a floating-point value between 0.0 and 1.0. This method can be used to create a series of random number selections, like a lottery draw, and is popular for producing random effects within Web pages.

Multiplying the random number will specify a wider range so, for example, a multiplier of 10 will create a random number now between 0.0 and 10.0.

To make the randomly generated number more useful it is generally best to round up the returned float so that the range will become two integer values.

The **Math.ceil()** method will be used to round the random number up to an integer between 1 and 10 inclusive.

The code below illustrates this example:

random.js

```javascript
// get a random number from 0.0 to 1.0
var rand1 = Math.random();
// multiply by 10 to make it between 0.0 and 10.0
var rand2 = rand1 * 10;
// round it up to make it between 1 and 10
var rand3 = Math.ceil( rand3 );

// add each part to a string
var str = "Random float [rand1]: " + rand1 + "\n";
str += "Specify range [rand2]: " + rand2 + "\n";
str += "Random integer [rand3]: " + rand3;

// display the string
alert(str);
```

*The individual steps are shown here with the **rand** variables but these can be combined as:*
Math.ceil(Math.random()*10)

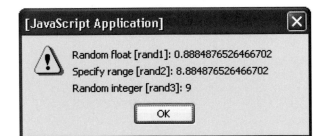

[JavaScript Application]

> Random float [rand1]: 0.8884876526466702
> Specify range [rand2]: 8.884876526466702
> Random integer [rand3]: 9
>
> OK

Lottery picker

This example uses **Math.random()** to generate a series of six random numbers within the range of 1 to 49 which can be used as selections in the national British lottery:

lotto.js

```
// create variables
var i, rand, temp, str;

// create a new array of 50 elements
var nums = new Array(50);

// fill elements 1-49 with numbers 1-49
for(i = 1; i < 50; i++) nums[i] = i;

// algorithm to randomize these numbers
for(i = 1; i < 50; i++)
{
   rand = Math.ceil(Math.random() * 49 );
   temp = nums[i];
   nums[i] = nums[rand];
   nums[rand] = temp;
}

// add the first six elements to a string
str = "Your six lucky numbers are:\n\n";
for(i = 1; i < 7; i++)
{
   str += nums[i];
   if(i != 6) str += " - ";
}

// display the string
alert(str);
```

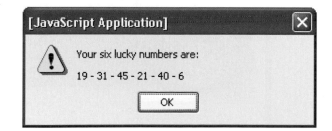

Random images

The **Math.random()** method is used in the following example to randomly select one of six images to be displayed in a Web page. The JavaScript displays an image, for an HTML **<img>** tag with a **id** attribute of **pic**. The image to display is determined by the code each time the page is loaded, and the script is executed.

It is important to remember that the **<script>** element to include this JavaScript must appear in the body of the HTML document after the **<img>** tag. Otherwise the code will be unable to find any element with an **id** of **pic** – so it will be unable to assign the randomly selected image.

rand-img.js

```
// create a new array and assign images to 6 elements
var pix = new Array;
pix[0] = "pic0.gif";
pix[1] = "pic1.gif";
pix[2] = "pic2.gif";
pix[3] = "pic3.gif";
pix[4] = "pic4.gif";
pix[5] = "pic5.gif";

// get a random integer between 0 and 5
var rand = Math.floor(Math.random() * 6);

// assign random image to the HTML <img> tag of pic id
document.getElementById("pic").src = pix[ rand ];
```

Document properties and methods are fully explained in Chapter 10.

Use this script to randomly display banners on a Web page.

Working with strings

This chapter explains string characteristics and demonstrates by example how text strings may be manipulated with JavaScript code.

Covers

Chapter Seven

String length

A string in JavaScript is simply zero or more characters enclosed within quotes, so these are all strings:

```
var str1 = "My First String";

var str2 = "";

var str3 = "2";

var str4 = "null";
```

The empty quotes in **str2** define the variable as being a **string** data type regardless of the empty string value. The numeric value assigned to **str3** is automatically converted to a **string** type when enclosed in quotes and the JavaScript **null** keyword is just a string literal when enclosed by quotes.

Spaces are counted as a character, too.

Essentially a string is a collection of characters, each character containing its own data, just like elements in a defined array.

It is logical to regard a string as an array of characters and apply array characteristics when using strings.

The example below parallels the **array.length** property with the **string.length** property:

string-length.js

```
// create and initialize a string variable
var a = "JavaScript Strings";

// display the length of the string
alert("String length is " + a.length );
```

```
[JavaScript Application]

⚠  String length is 18

        OK
```

Characters in strings

Strings are just arrays where each element is a character and can be referenced in the same way as regular array elements.

So just like arrays the first character is element 0 (zero).

The characters can be found using the **string.charAt()** method which takes the element index number as its sole argument.

The example below reads the characters in a string and makes changes according to the character found:

char-at.js

```
// create and initialize two string variables
var str = "linger in", newstr = "";

// get the first and last letters of the str variable
var a = "First letter : " + str.charAt(0);
var z = "Final letter : " + str.charAt( str.length -1 );

// loop through each character and copy into newstr
// unless it's an i - then copy an o into newstr
for( var i = 0; i < str.length; i++ )
{
    if( str.charAt(i) != "i" ) newstr += str.charAt(i);
    else newstr += "o";
}

// display newstr and the first and last letters of str
var result = "STRINGS\n\n";
result += "New string : " + newstr + "\n";
alert( result + a + "\n" + z );
```

This method can be used for simple string validation of an email address by seeking an @ character.

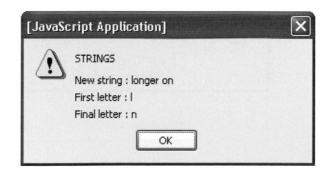

Join strings

The **+** operator is used to concatenate strings and is widely used in the example code given throughout this book.

A new string is created that consists of the first string followed immediately by the second string.

The example below concatenates a number of variable values into a single string, irrespective of the original data type – because JavaScript performs automatic data type conversion:

concat.js

```
// create and initialize an integer variable
var num = 99;

// create and initialize a float variable
var flt = 98.6;

// create and initialize a boolean variable
var bool = true;

// create and initialize several string variables
var str1 = "Although ";
var str2 = " F is cited as \"body temperature\" ";
var str3 = "\nthe ";
var str4 = " range is from about 97 to ";
var str5 = " F.";

// display the concatenated string
alert( str1 +flt +str2 +str3 +bool +str4 +num +str5 );
```

Remember to escape quotes if included inside a string.

[JavaScript Application]

⚠ Although 98.6 F is cited as "body temperature" the true range is from about 97 to 99 F.

OK

Search a string

JavaScript can search a string to find a character or substring passed as the argument to the **string.indexOf()** method.

If a match is made the method returns the starting position of the first occurrence of the matched character or substring within the searched string.

In the event that no match is found the **string.indexOf()** method returns a value of -1.

The following example uses the **string.indexOf()** method to seek a dot and **@** character within an email address string to perform a simple format validation:

isvalid.js

```
// create an initialize a string to search
var str= "mailme@domain.com";

// seek @, dot and # characters within the string
var att = str.indexOf("@");
var dot = str.indexOf(".");
var hsh = str.indexOf("#");

// make valid only if an @ and a dot are found
var fmt = ((att != -1)&&(dot != -1))? "valid":"invalid";

// display the results of the search
var res = "Format is " +fmt;
res += "\n@ at " +att;
res != "\nDot at " +dot;
res += "\n\nHash is " +hsh;
alert(res);
```

An optional second integer argument may specify the position from which to start the search.

[JavaScript Application]

⚠ Format is valid
@ at 6
Dot at 13

Hash is -1

OK

Separate words

The contents of a string may be separated using the JavaScript **string.split()** method.

A single argument should specify a common character for a delimiter at which points the string will be separated. Most commonly this can be a single space character so that a phrase with normal spacing will be separated into an array of single words.

Each of the words can then be referenced using the index number of the split string array, like any other array.

The example below illustrates this use of the **string.split()** method together with another instance where items in a database may use a | pipe character as the delimiter:

split.js

Data is often stored as a comma-delimited string.

```javascript
// create and initialize a string variable
var str = "JavaScript in easy steps";

// split words into array elements delimited by a space
var ss = str.split( " " );

// create and initialize another string variable
var bk = "JavaScript in easy steps|Mike McGrath";

// split words into array elements delimited by a pipe
var bks  = bk.split("|");

// display some split elements
var res = "Topic : " +  ss[0];
res += "\nTitle : " + bks[0];
res += "\nAuthor : " + bks[1];
alert(res);
```

Substrings

A substring may be extracted from an existing string using the **string.substring()** method which must have two arguments to specify the start and end positions of the required substring within the main string.

The character at the start argument position will be the first character in the returned substring. The last character in the substring will be the character preceding the given end argument position.

An alternative way to extract a substring from a string is available with the **string.substr()** method which also requires two arguments. While the first argument again specifies the start position of the substring the second will specify the length of the substring to be returned.

The example below demonstrates both substring methods:

substring.js

```
// create and initialize a string variable
var str = "JavaScript in easy steps";

// get two substrings with the substring() method
var sub1 = str.substring(14,19) +  str.substring(0,11)

// get two substrings with the substr() method
var sub2 = str.substr(14,5) + str.substr(0,10);

// display all the substrings
var res = "Substring method : " +sub1;
res += "\nSubstr method : " +sub2;
alert(res);
```

*The **substr()** method will invariably be easiest to use.*

[JavaScript Application]

⚠ Substring method : easy JavaScript
Substr method : easy JavaScript

OK

Convert to string

It is possible to manually call the JavaScript function that is used to convert other data types to strings by calling the **object.toString()** method.

This is an essential JavaScript function and will always try to return a string representation of the object that is being queried, even if it is not itself a string.

In this example there is firstly a straightforward addition of two integers, followed by a concatenation of a string with an integer where the integer is converted to a string value.

Finally the **object.toString()** method is demonstrated with a different data type to illustrate that the generated output will reveal the object type.

convert.js

*The **toString()** method can be used anywhere in JavaScript to reveal string information about any object.*

```javascript
// create an integer variable and add another integer
var num = 9;
var nostr = num + 9;

// create a string version of the num integer variable
// then concatenate a second value to it
var adstr= num.toString() + 9;

// create a new Image object
var img = new Image();

// display string values of the variables
var res = "No strings : " + nostr;
res += "\nAdded strings : " + adstr;
res += "\nImage : " + img.toString();
alert(res);
```

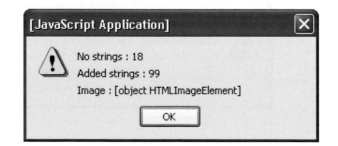

[JavaScript Application]

No strings : 18
Added strings : 99
Image : [object HTMLImageElement]

OK

Change case

The string character case may be changed using the **string.toUpperCase()** or **string.toLowerCase()** methods to force all the characters to become a common case.

Be sure to observe correct capitalization when using these methods.

These methods are useful when comparing user input to ensure that the character format agrees with the comparison format.

In the following example the function is called when the user clicks the button by assigning the function name to the **onclick** attribute of the button's HTML element, like this:

```
<input type="button" value="Check Input"
                    onclick="check_input()"/>
```

The **string.toLowerCase()** method converts the uppercase entry in the form text field for comparison with a lowercase string value.

case.js

```
function check_input()
{
  // get user input from text field in form id of f
  var entry = document.forms.f.textfield.value;

  // compare input and display an appropriate message
  if(entry.toLowerCase() == "castle") alert("Accepted");
  else alert("Refused");
}
```

See page 125 for fuller details on referencing form elements.

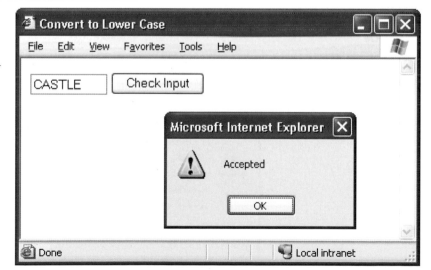

Numbers from strings

A number can be extracted from the beginning of a string with the **parseInt()** and **parseFloat()** methods.

The **parseInt()** method parses the string and returns the first integer value that is located. The **parseFloat()** method works in the same way but returns a floating point number.

If the parser finds any non-numeric character before returning a number then it will return the special **NaN** value that is used to denote "Not-a-Number".

This example demonstrates both **parseFloat()** and **parseInt()** methods and illustrates the JavaScript **isNaN()** function testing for a **NaN** value:

parse.js

*The **NaN** value cannot be tested for with the == equality operator.*

```javascript
// create a string beginning with a number
var str = "66.6% PASS RATE";

// extract the initial integer value
var res = "Integer : " + parseInt(str);

// extract the initial float value
res += "\nFloat : " + parseFloat(str);

// create a string beginning with a letter
var badstr = "PASS RATE 66.6%";

// attempt to extract an initial integer value
res += "\nNon-numeric : " + parseInt(badstr);
res += "\nFound : ";
res += isNaN( parseInt(badstr) )? "Character": "Number";
alert(res);
```

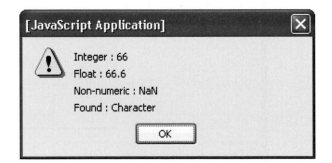

[JavaScript Application]

Integer : 66
Float : 66.6
Non-numeric : NaN
Found : Character

OK

Variables in strings

The JavaScript **eval()** function accepts as an argument a string containing JavaScript code which it evaluates, then returns the resulting value.

If the code string contains statements they will be executed by the **eval()** function, then the final value will be returned.

The *<script>* *element to include this JavaScript must appear in the HTML document after the form elements – so that the text field is created before the script can assign a value to it.*

While this function is a powerful feature of the JavaScript language it is most often used to introduce variable values into a string.

In the example below the script assigns a string value to be displayed in a text input within a form that simply has the **id** of **f**. The HTML <input> element has been named **textfield**.

The text box name and the display string are stored in variables that are evaluated by the **eval()** function.

eval.js

```javascript
// store the text input name
var inputname = "textfield";

// store the string to assign
var inputtext = " \"JavaScript Text\" ";

// evaluate the assignation expression
eval("document.forms.f."+inputname+".value="+inputtext);
```

Remember to escape the quotes inside a string to avoid error messages.

Now the text string is displayed in the text field because the expression evaluates to:

```javascript
document.forms.f.textfield.value = "JavaScript Text";
```

Encoding strings

All characters have a Unicode numerical representation that can be returned for each individual character in a string with the **string.charCodeAt()** method. This method requires the index of the character within the string as its argument.

Conversely characters can be extracted from Unicode using the JavaScript **String.fromCharCode()** function that takes the Unicode numeric value as its argument.

The example below first loops through a string and makes a comma delimited string of its Unicode character values. An array of these Unicode numeric values is then created for the second loop to return the character for each number:

unicode.js

```
// create and initialize three strings
var str = "Code Fun", enc = "", unc = "";

// get the str Unicode numbers, comma delimited
for( var i = 0; i < str.length; i++ )
{
   enc += str.charCodeAt( i ) + ",";
}

// split the list of numbers into array elements
var ss = enc.split( "," );

// convert the Unicode values back to characters
for( i = 0; i < ss.length; i++ )
{
   unc += String.fromCharCode( ss[i] );
}

alert( "Encoded : " +enc+ "\nUnencoded : " +unc );
```

Notice that the fromCharCode() function is a property of the String() constructor and is not a string object method.

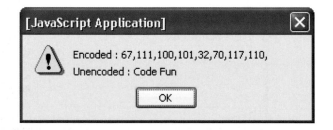

[JavaScript Application]

Encoded : 67,111,100,101,32,70,117,110,
Unencoded : Code Fun

OK

Addressing page objects

Following on from the JavaScript language foundation this chapter starts to explore how scripts may communicate with various aspects of a Web page using the browser Document Object Model (DOM).

Covers

Chapter Eight

Object constructor

The JavaScript syntax to address object properties and methods uses the object name followed by a period then the property name.

For instance, **array.length** addresses the **length** property of the **array** object.

To declare a property use both the object name and given property name.

Previous example code in this book has used intrinsic JavaScript objects with pre-defined properties and methods.

New custom objects can easily be created though using the JavaScript **new** keyword with the **Object()** constructor.

Properties may then be allocated to the new custom object by declaring a property name and assigning a value to it.

The example below creates a new object called **car** and then gives it three properties with assigned values:

object.js

```javascript
// create a new car object
var car = new Object();

// create and initialize a maker property
car.maker = "Porsche";

// create and initialize a model property
car.model = "Boxster";

// create and initialize a color property
car.color = "Red";

// display all the car property values
alert( car.color + " " + car.maker + " " + car.model );
```

Property inheritance

Further flexibility can be added to the example on the facing page by assigning the newly created custom object to a property of another custom object.

In this case the properties and values of the assigned object are inherited by the property of the second custom object.

The inherited properties are addressed by adding a period and the inherited property name after the property address to which they have been assigned.

It is helpful to understand this relationship when dealing with objects and properties in Web pages.

The following example demonstrates how a new object is assigned to a property of a second custom object and how the inherited properties may then be addressed:

inherit.js

```
// create a new object with assigned property values
var suv = new Object();
suv.badge = "Explorer";
suv.type = "4X4";
suv.doors = 4;
suv.color - "Red";
suv.engine = "4.0 liters";

// create another object that inherits from the first
var car = new Object();
car.maker = "Ford";
car.model = suv;

// display unique value and inherited property values
alert(car.maker+" "+car.model.badge+" "+car.model.type);
```

An object must have first been created in the script before it can be assigned to another object's property.

[JavaScript Application] ✕

⚠ Ford Explorer 4X4

OK

DOM hierarchy

The browser Document Object Model (DOM) is a collection of objects in a Web browser that can be addressed by JavaScript in order to influence the performance of a HTML document.

A fuller picture of DOM hierarchy is depicted on page 178 of this book.

These objects follow a strict hierarchy where the **window** object is the very top level. Because **window** is the top level "root" object it can be omitted in the address syntax. For instance, the **window.document.bgColor** property, which stores the value of the window's current background color, can be addressed simply as **document.bgColor**.

Several of the DOM objects have properties that contain an array of the elements in that Web page. For example, with **document.images[]**, the **images[]** array is a property of the **document** object that will store the URL address of each image contained on that Web page. The URL of the first image in the HTML code is stored in the array at **document.images[0]** then the URL of successive images are stored at incrementing array element index numbers.

The **set_bg()** function in the example below is called from the **onload** attribute of the HTML **<body>** tag to assign a value to the **document.bgColor** after the document has been loaded. This then sets the background color of the document to the specified value.

dom.js

```
// function to set the document background color
function set_bg()
{
    document.bgColor = "orange";
}
```

Simple DOM example

| File | Edit | View | Favorites | Tools | Help |

Done   Local intranet

Revealing page objects

The script example below reveals the default **window** object properties in both Internet Explorer 6.0 and Netscape 7.0.

```javascript
// show all window properties
for( propertyName in window )
  document.write( propertyName + ", " );
```

properties.js

*This script can show further DOM object properties – try replacing **window** with **document** to see all the **window.document** properties.*

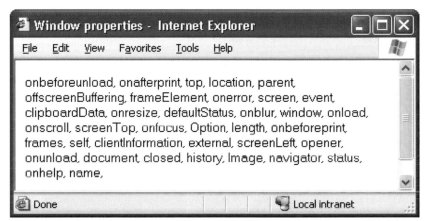

Browser ID

The **navigator** object has properties that provide information about the browser that is being used to view a document.

The browser name is revealed by the **navigator.appName** property whereas a description of that particular version is available from the **navigator.userAgent** property.

In addition to the release number the **navigator.userAgent** property contains other details, such as the host platform type.

In the example below the navigator-userAgent property reveals the browsers to be Internet Explorer 6.0 (MSIE 6.0) and Netscape 7.0 running on a Windows XP platform (NT5.1):

browser.js

```javascript
// get the browser name
var browser = navigator.appName;

// get the browser description
var description = navigator.userAgent;

// display the browser name and version
alert( browser + "\n\n" + description );
```

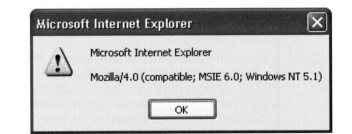

Cross-browser compliancy

In order for Web pages to display as desired it is sometimes necessary to identify the Document Object Model (DOM) which that browser supports.

Release 4.0 of both Netscape and Internet Explorer browsers added DOM support for dynamic HTML (DHTML). For this purpose Netscape introduced the **document.layers** property and Microsoft introduced the **document.all** property.

As Web browsers are free software the overwhelming majority of browsers now in use support the W3C DOM.

More recently, release 6.0 of Netscape and release 5.0 of Internet Explorer introduced support for a DOM devised by the World Wide Web Consortium (W3C). Crucially, this added a method called **document.getElementById()** that can be used to reference a HTML element on a page by the name assigned to its **id** attribute. For instance, **document.getElementById("pic")** could be used to reference a HTML element with an **id** value of **"pic"**. For example, **<img id="pic" src="pic.gif" alt="Fascinating Picture"/>**.

It is convenient to test for the existence **document.layers**, **document.all** and **document.getElementsById()** to discover which DOM is supported by the browser:

dom-test.js

```
// cross-browser DOM test
if(document.getElementById) alert("W3C DOM Supported");
else
if (document.all) alert("MSIE 4 DOM Supported");
else
if (document.layers) alert("NN 4 DOM Supported");
else alert("This is a really old Web browser");
```

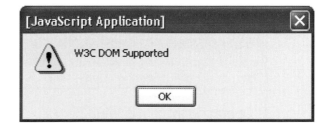

Platform check

The performance of a Web page may be affected by the operating system on which the browser is running due to some lack of support for the page content.

For example, a Web browser running on a Linux platform will not support Microsoft ActiveX controls. So any Web page containing an ActiveX control will not perform as intended on that platform.

Platform-specific scripting can be achieved, in a similar manner to that used for browser-specific scripting, with the **navigator.platform** property.

This property contains a short string representing the user's operating system and can be read to branch the script to accommodate any platform limitations.

The example below writes out the **navigator.platform** value:

platform.js

```javascript
// get the operating system type
var os = navigator.platform;

document.write("Operating system is " + os);
```

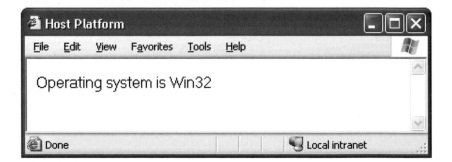

Plugins information

On Netscape/Mozilla browsers JavaScript can be used to discover information about any plugins that are installed in the browser with the **navigator.plugins** array property.

navigator.plugins exists in Internet Explorer but it's not implemented.

Each plugin that is installed within a Netscape/Mozilla browser is added as an element in the **navigator.plugins** array. For instance, if the Macromedia Shockwave plugin is installed there is a **navigator.plugins["Shockwave Flash"]** element.

The plugin element has a **name** property, storing the name and version of that plugin, and a **description** property that contains information about the plugin.

In the following example the JavaScript code first checks that the **navigator.appName** is Netscape before displaying the **name** and **description** of the first plugin in the **navigator.plugins** array:

plugins.js

```
// for Netscape/Mozilla browsers only
if(navigator.appName == "Netscape")
{
  // for the first plugin element
  with(navigator.plugins[0])
  {
    // display its name and description
    document.write("<h1>" +name+ "</h1>");
    document.write("<p>" +description+ "</p>");
  }
}
```

Mozilla browsers identify with the Netscape name.

The output from this script will vary according to the plugins installed on your browser.

Java detection

A browser can be assessed to discover if Java is enabled using the **navigator.javaEnabled()** method. This returns a boolean value of **true** or **false,** depending on the result.

The **navigator.javaEnabled()** method can be used to determine if a page containing a Java applet should be loaded, or if an alternative non-Java page should be loaded instead – as seen in this example:

java.js

```
// test if Java is enabled in the browser
if ( navigator.javaEnabled() )
{
  window.location = "javapage.html";  // if true go here
}
else
{
  window.location = "nojavapage.html"; // else go here
}
```

window.location stores the URL of the current page – assigning it a new URL will load that page in the browser. See page 100 for more about this property.

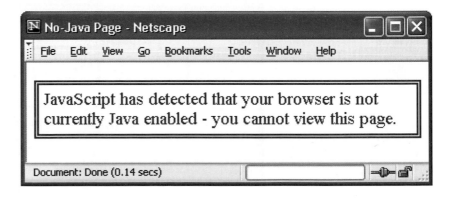

Window properties

This chapter demonstrates properties and methods of the **window** object. Creating pop-up windows is illustrated and the use of framed pages is also discussed with examples of how to address objects in other frames.

Covers

Chapter Nine

Confirm

The **alert()** function that is used extensively in the code examples given throughout this book is actually a method of the top-level **window** object, so may be correctly addressed as **window.alert()**.

The **window.confirm()** method is the first of two other **window** methods that produce dialog boxes when called.

It is used to get user confirmation from a dialog box containing an **OK** button that returns **true** to the script and a **Cancel** button that returns **false** to the script.

A single argument should be passed to the method as a text string containing the question for the user to confirm.

This example demonstrates the **window.confirm()** method performing conditional branching to determine which message string to write – depending upon which button the user pushes in the **confirm** dialog box:

confirm.js

*In this example **(ask)** is simply shorthand for **(ask == true)**.*

```
// create a variable to store a dialog response
var ask = confirm( "Do you wish to proceed ?" );

// create a variable to store a reply
var msg;

// assign an appropriate reply message
if( ask ) msg = "OK button was pushed";
else msg = "Cancel button was pushed";

// display the reply message
document.write( msg );
```

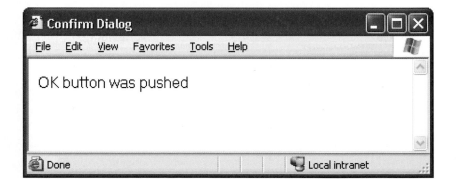

Prompt

The **window.prompt()** method is used to get keyboard input from the user through a dialog box containing a textfield together with **OK** and **Cancel** buttons.

Two string arguments are required by the **window.prompt()** method to specify a message to display and a default textfield value. The second argument should be an empty string if no default textfield value is needed by the script.

The dialog box returns the value of the textfield when the user presses the **OK** button. This example takes the user input to personalize the page:

prompt.js

```
/// request the user to enter their name
var user = prompt( "Please enter your name...", "" );

// provide a default name if field is left blank
if(user == null || user == "" ) user = "visitor";

// display a message with the user name
document.write( "Hi " +user+ ", welcome to this page");
```

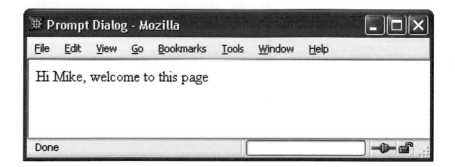

Location

The **window.location** object contains the full URL address of the document that is currently loaded in the browser.

It stores the actual full URL in the **window.location.href** property and assigning a new value to this, or to the **window.location** object itself, will load the specified URL into the browser.

A typical URL address may comprise these parts:

```
protocol: // host / pathname ? # hash
```

Each part of the URL address stored in the **window.location** object may be addressed individually using the appropriate location property – as demonstrated in this example:

location.js

Assigning a new value to **location.hash** *will move the browser to the given location in the page.*

```javascript
// assign each part of the current location to variables
var locn = "Href : " + location.href;

var prot = "Protocol : " + location.protocol;

var host = "Host : " + location.host;

var path = "Path : " + location.pathname;

var hash = "Hash : " + location.hash;

// display the variable values
alert(locn+"\n"+prot+"\n"+host+"\n"+path+"\n"+hash);
```

History

The **window.history** property contains an array of the URL addresses previously visited during a browser session. For security reasons these are not directly readable but they are used to navigate back to previous pages.

The **back()** and **forward()** methods of the **window.history** object emulate the browser's **Back** and **Forward** buttons.

More flexible navigation is often provided by the **window.history.go()** method that takes a single argument to specify the location by relative position. For instance, an argument value of **-1** will revisit the previous page and a value of **-2** reopens the page before it.

In a similar manner **window.history.go(1)** goes forward to the next page in the history array of visited URLs.

Calling **window.history.go(0)** causes the browser to reload the current document.

The function in the example below returns the user to the previous page. In this case the function is called from the **onclick** attribute of a button form input in the HTML document.

history-2.js

```
// a function to load the previous page
function go_back()
{
    window.history.go(-1);
}
```

Onload

The **window.onload** object may be used to specify the name of a function to be called immediately after a document has completely loaded in a browser.

Typically this initializing function is named **init()** and is often used to set a number of values within the script.

*The slideshow script on page 166 does not start to run until called by **onload** – after all the images have downloaded.*

It is especially useful when the page contains a large number of graphics that may take a while to download. If these images are used by the script it is essential that they finish downloading before the script starts to run.

The HTML **onload** attribute, that may optionally be included in the HTML **<body>** tag, can also set the **window.onload** object – so care is needed to avoid overwriting one with the other.

This is again the case with the **window.onunload** object and the HTML **<body>** tag's **onunload** attribute which can both specify a function to call when the user navigates to a new location.

Typically **window.onunload** calls a function that creates a pop-up window when the user leaves a website.

This example displays a simple **alert()** dialog message when the user exits the page:

onunload.js

```
// a function to display an exit message
function goodbye()
{
   alert("Thanks for calling - Come back soon");
}
```

The assigned value is the name of the function – the argument brackets are not required.

```
// specify the onunload event-handler
window.onunload = goodbye;
```

Status

The **window.status** object can be used to display a message in the status bar of the browser window until another feature in the displayed document sets a new status bar message, or the status bar is returned to its default state.

A default message to display can be specified with the **window.defaultStatus** object.

Discover more about **onmouseover** *and other events in Chapter 12.*

To display a message when the user places the cursor over a hyperlink the HTML **onmouseover** attribute should specify the message to display. It must also return **true** to prevent the link URL appearing in the status bar as it would do normally.

This example, using JavaScript within HTML tags, specifies a default message and adds an **onmouseover** attribute to the link. This displays another message while the cursor rests over the link:

status.html
(part of)

```
<body onload = "window.defaultStatus = 'Status Demo'" >

<p> <a href = "nextpage.html"
onmouseover = "window.status='Click Here';return true" >
Hypertext Link</a> </p>
```

Pop-up window

One of the most useful browser features provided by JavaScript is the ability to open a second browser window displaying another URL Web page.

This is possible using the **window.open()** method which takes three arguments to specify the URL to load in the pop-up window, a name for the pop-up and its desired dimensional features.

These pop-up windows are invariably smaller than the original window and have many uses including the display of large images from a display of thumbnail-sized images.

The example below opens a secondary pop-up window following complete loading of the first window:

popup-1.js

```
// a function to open a pop-up window
function popup()
{
  window.open( "popup-2.html", "",
"top=40,left=40,width=250,height=100");
}

// set the onload object
window.onload = popup;
```

The second argument must be an empty string if no name is being given to the pop-up window.

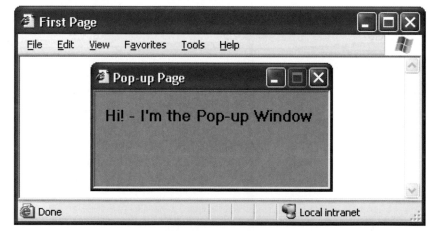

Pop-up features

The third argument to the **window.open()** method may specify many features to be included in the new window from the list in the following table:

Feature	Description
directories	Adds the links bar
height	Sets the height in pixels of the document area
left	The X co-ordinate of the window on the screen
location	Adds the address bar
menubar	Adds the standard menu bar
resizable	Permits the window to be resized
scrollbars	Enables scrollbars when needed
status	Adds the status bar
toolbar	Adds the button bar with back & forward buttons
top	The Y co-ordinate of the window on the screen
width	Sets the width in pixels of the document area

The list of features should have comma separators but no spaces.

The dimension features of **top**, **left**, **width** and **height** need to state a pixel value like the example on the facing page. All the other features can have a value of **yes** or **no** but if the feature appears in the argument a **yes** value is assumed – so it need not be specified.

For example, to add a status bar to the code on the facing page just requires the addition of **status** to the features list:

*popup-1.js
(amended)*

```
// a function to open a pop-up window with a status bar
function popup()
{
  window.open("popup-2.html", "",
  "top=40,left=40,width=250,height=100,status");
}
```

Close pop-up

A window can close itself simply by calling the **window.close()** method but closing a pop-up window requires a little more effort.

The initial call to the **window.open()** method should be assigned to a variable to create a **window** object. This new **window** object inherits the **window.close()** method which can close the pop-up.

This example verifies the existence of the pop-up window before closing it when the user exits the main window:

popup-close.js

```javascript
// create a variable to store a window object
var popwindow;

// a function to open a pop-up window
function popup()
{
  popwindow = window.open( "popup-2.html", "",
    "top=40,left=40,width=250,height=100,menubar,status");
}

// a function to close a pop-up window
function close_popup()
{
  if( popwindow != null ) popwindow.close();
}

// set the onload and onunload objects
window.onload = popup;
window.onunload = close_popup;
```

This pop-up page is the same as that in the example on page 104 – but now JavaScript has added status bar and menu bar features to this window.

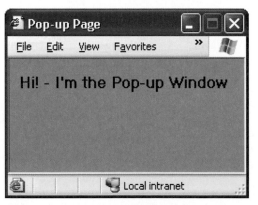

Get size

It is sometimes useful to have JavaScript get the user's screen resolution from the **width** and **height** properties of the **window.screen** object. Because a window may not be maximized to the full screen size it is also helpful to determine the actual inner width of the window.

The availHeight and availWidth properties of window.screen object contain the screen size excluding task bars.

The Netscape and Internet Explorer document object models have different ways of storing inner window dimensions so browser-specific scripting is needed.

In the example below window dimensions are retrieved from the appropriate object for each browser. The function is called by the **onload** attribute of the HTML **<body>** tag to ensure that the window has been created before seeking its dimensions.

size.js

```
function get_sizes()
{
  var win_w, win_h, scr_w, scr_h, res, inr;

  if(document.body.clientWidth)          // IE and Opera
  {
    win_w = document.body.clientWidth;
    win_h = document.body.clientHeight;
  }
  else if(window.innerWidth)    // Netscape and Mozilla
  { win_w = innerWidth; win_h = innerHeight; }

  scr_w = screen.width; scr_h = screen.height; // screen

  // display the size information
  res = "Resolution: " +scr_w+ " x " +scr_h;
  inr = "Inner window : " +win_w+ " x " +win_h;
  if(win_w != null) alert( res + "\n" + inr );
}
```

You can call the window.print() method to print out the document in the browser window.

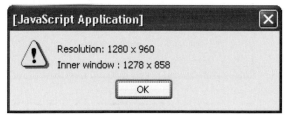

[JavaScript Application]

⚠ Resolution: 1280 x 960
Inner window : 1278 x 858

OK

Frames array

The **window.frames** object contains an array of all the frames in a window which have been defined in the HTML **<frameset>** tags.

JavaScript can address these from within any frame using the **parent.window.frames[]** array syntax.

Individual frames can be addressed using their index number in the array, or by the value assigned to the **name** attribute in the HTML **<frame>** tag. So a frame named **"main"** can be addressed from within another frame as **parent.window.frames["main"]**, or more simply as **parent.window.frames.main**.

The script below is included in a HTML frame document. It finds the total number of frames in that frameset and reads each of their names from the **parent** frame-holder document:

frame-1.js

Always name HTML elements to be used by JavaScript to produce code that is more comprehensible.

```
// find the total number of frames
var framenums = "No. frames :"
                + parent.window.frames.length;

// retrieve the name of each frame
var framenames= "\nFrame 1 : "
                + parent.window.frames[0].name;
framenames+= "\nFrame 2 : "
                + parent.window.frames[1].name;

framenames+= "\nFrame 3 : "
                + parent.window.frames[2].name;

alert( framenums + framenames );
```

Frame objects

The example on the facing page allows access to different frames within a framed window and because the browser DOM is hierarchical that means that the objects and properties within any frame are also accessible.

The script can assign values to these object properties and use their methods just as with an unframed window.

Typically a navigation frame on the left side of the window will have navigation buttons which, when pushed, will assign new URL locations to a main frame on the right side of the screen.

This example adds a further function to the code listed on the opposite page. This is called from the HTML **onclick** attribute of the button to write text in the **Banner** frame and to change the location of the **Page** frame:

frame-1.js
(addition to)

```
function next()
{
  // load another page into the Page frame
  parent.frames.Page.window.location = "nextpage.html";

  // write text into the Banner frame
  parent.frames.Banner.window.document.write
  ("Frame 2 - Written by Frame 1");
}
```

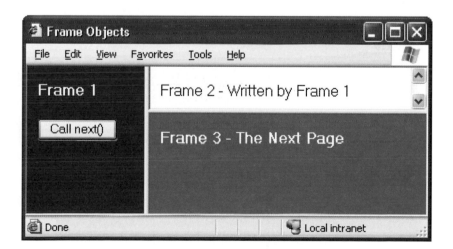

Error handling

A custom error-handling function may be assigned to the **window.onerror** object to deal with runtime errors.

When the browser meets an error it looks for an error-handler in the script but, if none is found, it will handle the error itself by opening the browser error dialog box.

Once the error has been notified a **true** value is returned to the browser to indicate that the error has been dealt with.

The error-handler must be declared at the top of the script to catch all possible errors.

To avoid all error dialogs a custom error-handler function need only return **true** when an error is encountered.

Usefully the browser will pass three arguments to the error-handler containing information on the nature of the error, the URL of the file that contains the error, and the actual line number in that file where the error exists.

In the example below each piece of error information passed to the error-handling function by the browser is displayed for the user:

error.js

```
// declare an error-handling function
window.onerror = errorhandler;

// define the error-handling function
function errorhandler( msg, url, ln )
{
  alert("Error: "+msg+"\nIn File:"+url+"\nAt Line:"+ln);
  return true;    // tell the browser it's been handled
}

// This is a deliberate mistake
document.form[ theMistake ].value = "myButton";
```

[JavaScript Application]

⚠ Error: theMistake is not defined
In File:http://localhost/error.js
At Line:12

OK

Document properties

This chapter illustrates properties and methods of the **window.document** object. Image-swapping rollovers are demonstrated and cookies are explained. There is also an overview of how layers are used in JavaScript.

Covers

Chapter Ten

Set colors

The window. part of the address may be omitted as window is the top level DOM object.

The properties and methods of the **window.document** object enable a Web page document to be changed at runtime. Using JavaScript to assign new values to properties of the **window.document** object causes the Web browser to update the appearance of the Web page in line with the new values.

This can be simply illustrated by assigning new values to the **document.bgColor** and **document.fgColor** properties to change the background and foreground colors of a page.

In this example the **set_colors()** function is called from the HTML **onclick** attribute of the button when the user pushes it:

colors.js

```
// a function to set the colors of the page
function set_colors()
{
  window.document.bgColor = "red";
  window.document.fgColor = "yellow";
}
```

Notice the capitalization with both bgColor and fgColor.

JavaScript creates

The **write()** method of the **window.document** object is a tremendously powerful feature that allows JavaScript to create content dynamically when loading a Web page.

The method takes a single string argument containing the content to be written into the page and this may include HTML tags to format the content.

Using **write()** JavaScript can dynamically create layers – see page 121.

Typically the **document.write()** method appears within a script in the **<body>** section of a HTML document and will write selected content following a conditional test.

It should be noted that calling this method at runtime will cause the specified content to be written into a new blank document so replacing the current page.

Variable values may also be concatenated with a string argument in order to introduce a variable value into the content of a Web page.

This example first generates a random number then tests to determine if the number is odd or even. Selected content is added to the page depending on the result of this test:

write.js

```
// get a random integer between 1 - 100
var n = Math.ceil( Math.random() * 100 );

// determine whether the number is odd or even
var ntype = ( n % 2 == 0 ) ? "Even" : "Odd";

// write a description of the number
document.write("<h1>Number " +n+ " is " +ntype+"</h1>");
```

![Write Content browser window displaying: Number 87 is Odd]

Set cookie

Cookies are tiny files that can be written by JavaScript to store small amounts of data on the local hard drive. There are limitations to the use of cookies that restrict their size to 4 kilobytes and Web browsers are not required to retain more than 20 cookies per Web server. Typically a cookie may often retain user data for use across Web pages or on subsequent visits to a website.

Escape the values to include spaces, commas and semicolons.

The cookie data is held in the **window.document.cookie** object as a **name=value** pair – the value may not contain any semicolons, commas or whitespace. Multiple **name=value** pairs may be stored by making further assignations to the **document.cookie** object.

The life-span of a cookie is limited to the length of the current browser session unless an expiry date is specified when the cookie is first set.

Expiration is assigned to a key named **expires** by amending a current **Date** object to the desired future date.

A cookie may be deleted by setting an expiry date that is before the real current date.

Dates of expiry should be expressed in GMT string format by converting the amended **Date** object using the **Date.toGMTString()** method.

The calculation in the example below multiplies the days, hours, minutes, seconds and milliseconds to increment a **Date** object by exactly 1 week.

This example stores the user's name and account number in a cookie with a life-span of 7 days:

set-cookie.js

```
// the data to be stored in the cookie
var user_account = "Mike McGrath,000456";

// create a new Date object
var expiry = new Date();

// set the expiry for 7 days time
expiry.setTime( expiry.getTime() + (7*24*60*60*1000) );

// create the cookie
document.cookie = "cookiedata="+escape(user_account)+";"
+ "expires=" +expiry.toGMTString()+ ";" ;
```

Get cookie

If a cookie is set the **document.cookie** object will return **true** so JavaScript can test for the presence of cookies. When a cookie is located the **document.cookie** object returns the stored data string. Parts of the data may be retrieved from the stored string using the regular string manipulation methods covered earlier in this book.

When the script below runs it first seeks the cookie set by the previous example on the opposite page, then it extracts the data values to write customized dynamic content:

Unescape any escaped data when retrieving from cookies.

get-cookie.js

```
// find any cookies
if( document.cookie )
{
  // unescape the cookie data
  var cookiedata = unescape( document.cookie );
  // split the name=value pairs
  var userdata = cookiedata.split( "=" );
  // if the cookie is called cookiedata
  if( userdata[0] == "cookiedata" )
  {
    // split the comma delimited values
    var data = userdata[1].split( "," );
    var username = data[0];
    var useracct = data[1];
  }
}
// write out the data retrieved from the cookie
document.write("Welcome " +username+ "<br/>");
document.write("Account number: " +useracct+ ".");
```

Multiple **name=value** *pairs will automatically be returned with a semicolon separating each pair. Use* **string.indexOf()** *to identify the required pair.*

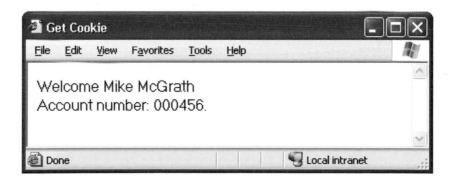

Images array

The **window.document.images[]** object is an array of all image objects contained within a Web page – in the order in which the HTML code added them to the page. So the first listed image is allocated to the first array element and can be addressed as **document.images[0]**.

Always give images a name with the HTML **id** *attribute.*

In this example the name assigned to the HTML **id** attribute and the **src** URL can be accessed for each image along with the total length of the **document.images** array:

*The **images** array elements are only available after the browser has completely loaded the page.*

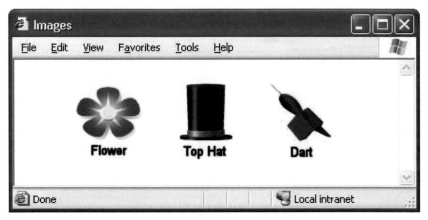

images.js

```javascript
// a function to get images information
function image_info()
{
 var msg = "Total Images : " + document.images.length;
 msg +="\nMiddle Image Name : "+document.images[1].id;
 msg +="\nMiddle Image Source: "+document.images[1].src;
 alert(msg);
}
```

This example assumes these images appear in the HTML code sequentially from left to right – but this may not always be the case.

Rollover

If an image has been named in the HTML code, by assigning a value to the **<img>** tag's **id** attribute, it may also be addressed by this name in JavaScript. The syntax is **document.images.*imgname*** – so an image named **click** is addressed as **document.images.click**.

*An **id** attribute should be a single-word name – without spaces.*

Assigning a new value to the **src** property of an image causes the browser to replace the image. Typically this is seen in rollovers – when the cursor is over an image it is replaced by a second image, the original image is returned when the cursor moves away. The HTML **<img>** tag must include an **onmouseover** attribute and an **onmouseout** attribute to create a rollover effect, like this:

```
<img id="click" src="off.gif" alt=""
   onmouseover="swap(1)" onmouseout="swap(0)" />
```

These attributes call the JavaScript image-swapping function whenever the **onmouseover** or **onmouseout** events occur:

rollover.js

```
function swap(n)
{
  if( n == 0 )document.images.click.src = "off.gif";
  if( n == 1 )document.images.click.src = "over.gif";
}
```

Preload the swap image to avoid download delay (see page 52) and only use images of like dimensions.

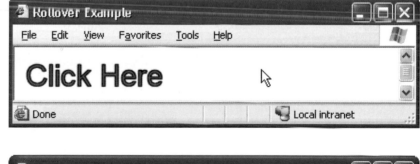

Dynamic content

The **window.document.open()** method opens a new HTML document which can be written to using the familiar method **window.document.write()** to create dynamic content.

When the content has been written the document stream should be closed by the **window.document.close()** method.

The example below builds on the pop-up window example in the last chapter by writing the content from JavaScript instead of simply loading an existing HTML document:

dynamic-popup.js

```javascript
// a function to create a dynamic popup window
function popup()
{
 // create the popup window
 var popwindow =
 window.open("","","top=40,left=30,width=250,height=125");
 // open the pop-up window HTML document
 popwindow.document.open();
 // write content in the pop-up window
  popwindow.document.write("<title>Pop-up</title>");
popwindow.document.write("Dynamic Pop-up Page<br/>");
 popwindow.document.write("<img src='dex.gif' alt=''>");
 // remember to finally close the HTML document
 popwindow.document.close();
}
```

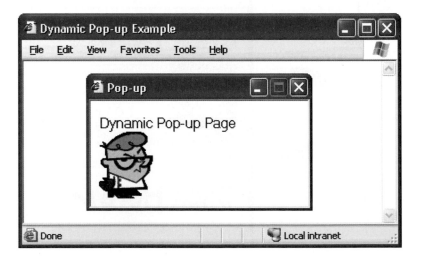

Last modified

The **window.document.lastModified** object can provide date and time information of when a Web page was last updated. This data is usually supplied to **document.lastModified** from the HTTP file header that is sent by the Web server. In some instances the Web server may omit this information so **document.lastModified** will, in those cases, return zero.

Typically this data is used to indicate how recently a Web page has been updated so the user knows how current the information on that page may be. Usually this information is displayed at the bottom of a page in a smaller font than the general page text.

The example that follows first tests that a date has been supplied to **document.lastModified** then writes the data into the HTML document:

last-modified.js

```
// check that there is a lastModified date
if( Date.parse( document.lastModified ) != 0 )

// if so, write a message stating what that date is
document.write
( "Page last updated: " + document.lastModified );
```

The <script> block to include this script code would normally be situated at the very end of the HTML document <body> section.

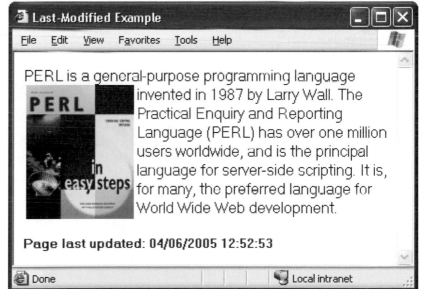

Last-Modified Example

PERL is a general-purpose programming language invented in 1987 by Larry Wall. The Practical Enquiry and Reporting Language (PERL) has over one million users worldwide, and is the principal language for server-side scripting. It is, for many, the preferred language for World Wide Web development.

Page last updated: 04/06/2005 12:52:53

XYZ coordinates

Physical position of content in a display window can be referred to using coordinates called X, Y and Z.

The X coordinate specifies the distance in pixels from the extreme left edge of the window.

The Y coordinate specifies the distance in pixels from the extreme top edge of the window.

The Z coordinate specifies the stacked position, by index number, of layers above the bottom window level:

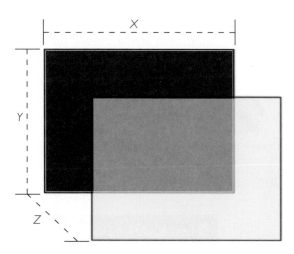

To differentiate the coordinates remember that "a cross" (X) means "across".

The X coordinate at the left edge of the window is zero and the Y coordinate at the top edge of the window is also zero.

A position where X=50 and Y=30 would pinpoint a location 50 pixels from the left edge and 30 pixels from the top edge.

The Z coordinate of the bottom window level has an index value of zero. Layers may be placed over this level, like transparent sheets, and are given unique Z-index values.

A window may have many layers but the top layer will always have the highest Z-index value. Each successive layer below that will have a decreasingly lower Z-index value.

Dynamic layers

JavaScript can create layers dynamically by writing the necessary HTML code and stylesheet rules into the body section of the HTML document. This allows control over the position and appearance of each layer.

Most importantly, if layers overlap each other their stacking order can be determined by the value assigned to their **z-index** property – the higher the number, the higher the layer will be in the stack.

The example below emulates the illustration on the opposite page by dynamically creating two overlapping layers. The second (yellow) layer is higher in the stack than the first (purple) layer. If their **z-index** values were reversed, so **layer 1** was 20 and **layer 2** was 10, the purple layer would overlap the yellow layer.

layers.js

```
// write a layer at z-index 10
document.write("<div id='layer1'
style='position:absolute; top:20px; left:20px;
width:80px; height:80px; background-color:purple;
color:white; z-index:10; border:1px solid black'>
Layer #1</div>");
```

*The **<script>** element to include this script should be located in the body section of the HTML document.*

```
// write a layer at z-index 20
document.write("<div id='layer2'
style='position:absolute; top:40px; left:40px;
width:80px; height:80px; background-color:yellow;
z-index:20; border:1px solid black'>Layer #2</div>");
```

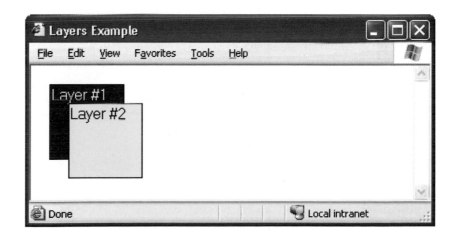

Transparent layers

Unless specified otherwise, a layer will usually be created with the same background as the document body – so will appear to be transparent. Alternatively it can be explicitly set to be transparent by setting its **background-color** property to **transparent**.

The transparency of layers is particularly important when they contain GIF images of irregular shapes that have transparent parts. On a transparent layer these images appear to simply float over the document background. Several images can appear in close proximity, even when their layers overlap, by allocating different **z-index** values to determine their stacking order.

The script below creates two such layers – but only one is transparent to illustrate the difference in how each image appears.

transparent-layers.js

```
// create a transparent layer
document.write("<div id='transparent-layer'
style='position: absolute; top:20px; left:230px;
width:75px; height:110px; background-
color:transparent'><img src='deedee.gif' alt=''></
div>");
```

```
// create a white layer
document.write("<div id='transparent-layer'
style='position: absolute; top:20px; left:315px;
width:75px; height:110px; background-color:white'><img
src='deedee.gif' alt=''></div>");
```

The image used in this example is in the GIF format and has its green color set to transparent. The image actually looks like this:

Form properties

This chapter illustrates how JavaScript can manipulate user input from HTML form elements. Examples are given for all common form input elements including radio buttons and selection boxes together with email address validation.

Covers

Chapter Eleven

The form object

The **window.document.forms** object contains an array of all the forms in a HTML document, indexed in the order in which they appear in the HTML code.

For instance, **window.document.forms[0]** addresses the first form to appear in the HTML code of a Web page.

If the **id** attribute of the **<form>** element has been assigned a value then the form can be addressed by name. So a form named **f** can simply be addressed as **document.forms.f**.

*The **enctype** attribute value is stored by the **encoding** property name. This property is read-only but all other properties may be assigned new values.*

All other attributes assigned in the **<form>** tag are also accessible as properties of that form object. For instance, with this form...

```
<form id = "f" method = "post" action = "mailto:a@b.com"
enctype = "text/plain">
```

...the following JavaScript function can be called from the HTML **<body>** tag's **onload** attribute to reveal the form properties:

form-properties.js

```
function form_info()
{
  // get the form name
  var msg = "Name: "   + document.forms.f.id;

  // get the form method, action and encoding type
  msg += "\nMethod: "  + document.forms.f.method;
  msg += "\nAction: "  + document.forms.f.action;
  msg += "\nEnctype: " + document.forms.f.encoding;
  alert(msg);
}
```

Form elements

The **window.document.forms[].elements** object contains an array of all the elements within a form indexed in the order in which they appear in the HTML code. With a form named **f** for instance, **document.forms.f.elements[0]** addresses the first element that appears in that form.

If the **name** attribute of the element has been assigned a value then the element can be addressed by name. So the element named **btn1** in this form **f** can simply be addressed as **document.forms.f.btn1**...

```
<form id = "f" method = "post" action = "">
<input type="button" name="btn1" value="Click Me"
onclick="alert('Hi - I am a button')"/> </form>
```

Other attributes are accessible as properties of that element – as illustrated by this example:

element-properties.js

*Unless stated otherwise, all the example functions in this chapter are called from the HTML **<body>** tag's **onload** attribute – a form field cannot be changed before it has been created.*

```
function element_info()
{
  // get the element type
  var msg = "Element Type: "+document.forms.f.btn1.type;
  // get the element value
  msg += "\nElement Value:
                "+document.forms.f.btn1.value;
  // get the element onclick
  msg += "\nElement Onclick: "
                +document.forms.f.btn1.onclick;
  alert( msg );
}
```

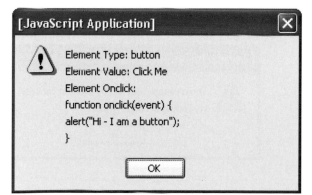

Click buttons

Values assigned in the HTML code may be reassigned by JavaScript so that a button will perform a different action.

In the example below a HTML **onclick** attribute specifies that the **first()** function will be called when the button is pushed:

```
<form id="f" method="post" action="">
<input type="button" name="btn1" value="Click Me"
onclick="first()"/> </form>
```

The **first()** function assigns a string to a variable, then specifies a new event-handler function called **second()** to the button's **onclick** attribute. Subsequently pushing the button will call the **second()** function and execute the statement it contains.

event-handlers.js

```
// create a global variable
var msg;

// a function to store an initial message
function first()
{
  msg = "This message was left by the first function";
  // assign another function to the button
  document.forms.f.btn1.onclick = second;
}
```

When assigning event-handler functions only assign the name – without any following brackets.

```
// a function to store a second message and display both
function second()
{
  msg += "\nHi, I\'m the second function";
  alert(msg);
}
```

Toggle value

It is useful to change the label that is displayed on a button by its **value** attribute if that button performs dual actions.

In the following example a button calls a **stopgo()** function to start or stop a counter. The counter increments an integer variable at 1-second intervals and displays the count in the window's status bar.

The button label normally reads **Start** but changes to **Stop** if the timer **count()** function is running.

toggle.js

*The **num** variable is initialized at -1 so that when first incremented the counter will start at zero.*

The ! operator is used here to change the boolean variable to the opposite of its current value.

```javascript
var running = false, num = -1, tim;       // create globals

function count()                          // counter function
{
  if(running)
  {
    num++;                                // increment the tally
    window.status = "Seconds elapsed: " + num;
    tim = setTimeout( "count()", 1000 );
  }
  else
  { num = -1; clearTimeout( tim ); }      // or halt
}

function stopgo()                         // control function
{
  running = !running;                     // toggle counter
  count();
  document.forms.f.btn1.value =
    (running)? "Stop" : "Start";          // change the label
}
```

Toggle Function -

File Edit View Favorites Tools Help

> Stop

Seconds elapsed: 15   Local intranet

Text boxes

The text displayed in a HTML text **<input>** is easily changed by JavaScript simply by assigning a new string to the **value** property of that form element.

Historically, text boxes were restricted to display text in just one fixed font but modern browsers allow a choice of font, size and color.

The example below displays a string in a text box and adds style characteristics for font, foreground-color and background-color:

text-field.js

```javascript
// a function to set the text in a form text field
function set_text()
{
  // for text field txt1 in form f
  with(document.forms.f.txt1)
  {
    // set the text value
    value = "JavaScript in easy steps";

    // set the style characteristics
    style.fontFamily = "comic sans ms";
    style.fontSize = "16pt";
    style.color = "yellow";
    style.backgroundColor ="red";
  }
}
```

Password boxes

A HTML password **<input>** is simply a text box that displays asterisks in place of the actual characters.

This example converts the string input by the user, into a password field named **pwd1**, to lowercase and assigns the string to a variable.

If the variable string matches the correct password then the browser will load the first page of the website – but it will display an **alert()** dialog message if the string does not match.

password-field.js

```
// a function to validate a password entry
function validate()
{
  // convert the input to lowercase
  var entry = document.forms.f.pwd1.value.toLowerCase();
  // relocate the browser if the input is correct
  if( entry == "admin") window.location = "page1.html";
  else
  {
    // display a message if the input is incorrect
    alert("Password incorrect - Please retry...");
    // clear the password field
    document.forms.f.pwd1.value = "";
  }
}
```

*The final line in this script will clear the password box after the user clicks the alert **OK** button, to be ready for another entry.*

Radio buttons

A group of radio buttons that will only allow one of the group to be checked at any time should all have the same name assigned to their name attribute in the HTML **<input>** tag.

In the browser DOM the radio button group creates a **document.form** object with that given name.

This object contains an array of all the radio buttons in the group, indexed in the order in which they appear in the HTML code.

JavaScript can address each radio button using the array name and index number. In the example below JavaScript checks the second radio button then displays both radio values in a text box:

radio-buttons.js

```
// a function to get radio group information
function radio_info()
{
  // select the second radio button
  document.forms.f.rad1[1].checked = true;

  // get both radio button values
  var msg = "1st Radio Value: "
  + document.forms.f.rad1[0].value;
  msg += "   2nd Radio Value: "
  + document.forms.f.rad1[1].value;
  document.forms.f.txt1.value = msg;
}
```

*Only checked radio buttons have their **name=value** pair sent when the form is submitted.*

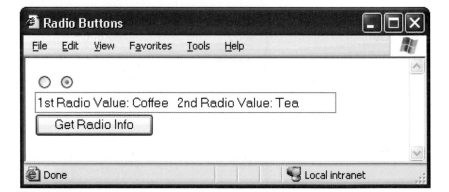

Radio polling

The important feature of a radio button is whether it is checked or not. This can be ascertained from the radio button's **checked** property that will return a boolean **true** if the radio is checked or a boolean **false** if it is unchecked.

JavaScript can loop through all the radio button array elements to test for a **true checked** property, then use the value assigned to the radio button that is checked.

In the example below the function is called from the HTML **onclick** attribute of the push button form **<input>**. This loops through the elements of the radio button array to discover which button, if any, is checked. When a button has been checked its associated value is used by the script to apply a new background color to the page.

radio-poll.js

In JavaScript
if(checked) *is shorthand for* ***if(checked==true)***.

```
// a function to discover which radio button is selected
function radio_poll()
{
  // loop through all radio buttons
  for(var i=0; i < document.forms.f.rad1.length; i++)
  {
    // if the radio is selected, use its value
    if( document.forms.f.rad1[i].checked )
    document.bgColor=document.forms.f.rad1[i].value;
  }
}
```

Checkboxes

Unlike radio buttons a checkbox operates independently from other checkboxes and so all checkboxes should be uniquely named by their **name** attribute in the HTML code.

Each checkbox creates a **document.form** object with its given name and, like a radio button, has a **checked** property.

In the following example the HTML **onclick** attribute of a button calls the JavaScript function that sets the **checked** property of three checkboxes:

checkboxes.js

Only those checkboxes that are checked will have their **name=value** *pairs sent to the server on submission of the form.*

```javascript
// a function to check three checkboxes
function checkall()
{
  // in the form named f
  with(document.forms.f)
  {
    // check checkboxes named chk1, chk2 and chk3
    chk1.checked = true;
    chk2.checked = true;
    chk3.checked = true;
  }
}
```

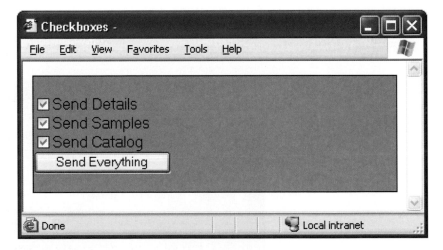

Checkbox polling

The **checked** property of a checkbox object is most important and JavaScript may test for checked checkboxes then use their associated values.

The example below tests the **checked** property of all checkboxes and assigns the **value** of those that are checked to a string variable for display in an **alert()** dialog box:

checkbox-poll.js

```javascript
// a function to discover which checkboxes are selected
function checkbox_poll()
{
  // create a string for the results
  var str = "Color choice is ";

  // loop through all checkboxes
  for( var i=1; i<4; i++ )
  {
    // if the checkbox is selected, add its value
    if( eval("document.forms.f.chk"+i+".checked") )
      str += eval("document.forms.f.chk"+i+".value+' '");
  }
  // display the results
  alert( str );
}
```

*Use the **eval()** function to combine form property names and numbers.*

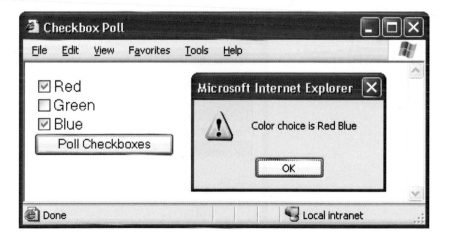

Option lists

The **<option>** items in a HTML **<select>** list have a **text** property for each displayed string label and an associated **value** property. These are equivalent to the HTML **name** and **value** attributes of each **<option>** element in the **<select>** list.

This **name=value** pair is sent to the server when the form is submitted.

All menu items are stored in the **<select>** object's **options[]** array and both the **text** name label and its associated **value** may be dynamically written by JavaScript.

This example dynamically sets the label **name** and the associated **value** of all three option items in a drop-down list. The form has the simple **id** of **f** and the **<select>** element has the **id** of **menu**.

options.js

*The **options[]** elements must be initially created by the HTML code.*

```
// a function to set the name and values of list options
function set_options()
{
  with( document.forms.f.menu )
  {
  options[0].text = "One"; options[0].value = "1";
  options[1].text = "Two"; options[1].value = "2";
  options[2].text = "Three"; options[2].value = "3";
  }
}
```

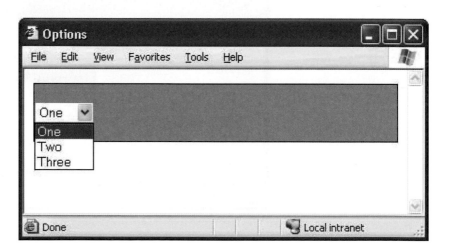

Selected index

An **options[]** array has a property called **selectedIndex** that contains the index number of the item currently selected.

JavaScript can most usefully retrieve the value of the current selection for dynamic effects.

This example extracts the value of the current selection for display in a text box. The form has the **id** of **f** and the **<select>** element has the **id** of **city**. The function is called by the **onclick** attribute of the button when the user clicks it.

selected.js

*This example could use a **with** statement to make the script more concise.*

```javascript
// a function to get the selected item in a list
function get_selected()
{

  // a variable to store the selected index number
  var pick = document.forms.f.city.selectedIndex;

  // assign the value of the selected element
  // to a text field with the id of txt1
  document.forms.f.txt1.value =
    document.forms.f.city.options[pick].value;
}
```

| Selected Option |
| File Edit View Favorites Tools Help |

New York ▾   Show Selected   New York
London
New York
Paris
Sydney

Done   Local intranet

Text areas

A HTML **<textarea>** element is rather like a large scrolling text box input whose value can be read and written by JavaScript.

The example below writes content to a text area by assigning a string to its **value** property after the document is loaded.

The function to assign the string is designated as the document's **onload** event handler by the script.

Care is needed when using this approach – if the script is included in the **<head>** section of the HTML document an **onload** attribute in the **<body>** tag may overwrite it.

textarea.js

*It is often best to call onload functions using the **onload** attribute of the HTML **<body>** element.*

```
// a function to write text content in a text area
function write_text()
{
  // assign a string to the textarea field
  document.forms.f.txtarea1.value = "Computers in the
future may perhaps only weigh 1.5 tons. (Popular
Mechanics forecasting the development of computer
technology, 1949)";
}

// define the onload function
window.onload = write_text;
```

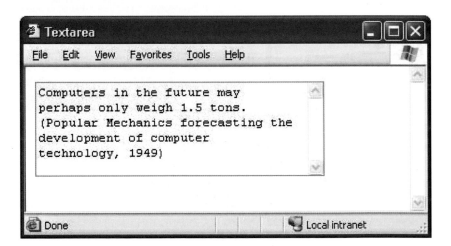

Clear form

The **reset()** method of a form object will reset all the values within the form and update the inputs to their original state – just as if the user had pushed a reset button. Careful use should be made of the **reset()** method to avoid the need for the user to input data repeatedly.

*See page 155 for an example of a **reset** confirmation using the **onreset** event.*

The example below uses the **javascript:** protocol to call the intrinsic JavaScript **reset()** function. This allows the user to click an image to reset the form, rather than a traditional reset button. Some short pieces of JavaScript can be inserted into a HTML document this way – without the need for any other script:

reset.html
(part of)

```
<form id="f" method="post" action="">
<p>
<input type="checkbox" name="chk1" value="fun"/>
Fun JavaScript<br/>
<input type="checkbox" name="chk2" value="great"/>
Great JavaScript<br/>
<input type="checkbox" name="chk3" value="easy"/>
Easy JavaScript<br/>
<img src="reset.gif" alt=""
 onclick="javascript:document.forms.f.reset()"/>
</p>
</form>
```

*See page 160 for more on the **javascript:** protocol.*

Send form

When a form is submitted to the server the values assigned to the **name** and **value** attributes of each form element are sent as **name=value** pairs.

The **submit()** method of the form object can be used to send the form to the server in exactly the same way as if the user had pushed a HTML submit button.

See page 160 for more on the *javascript:* protocol.

The example below uses the **javascript:** protocol to call the intrinsic JavaScript **submit()** function. This allows the user to click an image to submit a form, rather than a traditional submit button.

submit.html
(part of)

```
<form id="f" method="post" action="parser.cgi">
<p>
<input type="checkbox" name="chk1" value="fun"/>
Fun JavaScript<br/>
<input type="checkbox" name="chk2" value="great"/>
Great JavaScript<br/>
<input type="checkbox" name="chk3" value="easy"/>
Easy JavaScript<br/>
<img src="submit.gif" alt=""
 onclick="javascript:document.forms.f.submit()"/>
</p>
</form>
```

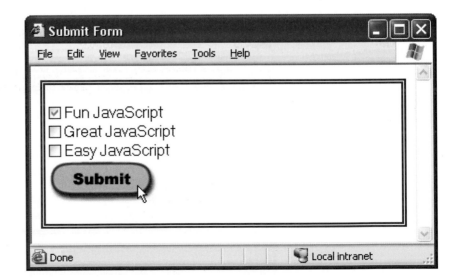

Amend form

The **onsubmit** property of a form object can be used to execute a JavaScript function just before the form data is sent to the server. This may be when the user pushes a HTML submit button, or when the form is sent with the form object's **submit()** method.

The function will be executed then the form will be submitted to the server. Usefully, this allows JavaScript to amend the form so that the **name=value** pairs can be better used by a receiving CGI script.

In the example below the HTML **onsubmit** attribute of the **<form>** element calls the **add_zeros()** function just before the form data is sent to the server. This function ensures that any empty text input element gets a zero value assigned to it:

onsubmit.js

```
// a function to assign zeros to empty text fields
function add_zeros()
{
  with(document.forms.f)
  {
    if(txt1.value == "") txt1.value = "0";
    if(txt2.value == "") txt2.value = "0";
    if(txt3.value == "") txt3.value = "0";
  }
}
```

The CGI script acknowledges the **name** fields and the zero values:

The illustration shows the user has entered a quantity for the **txt1** *field then clicked Submit – which has added the zeros from JavaScript.*

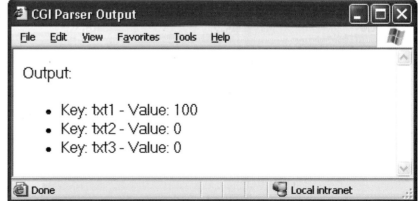

Email address validation

The value of form elements may be validated for correct format before the form is submitted.

In the following example JavaScript tests the format of a text input string for the presence of **@** and dot characters and will only submit the form if the email address validation appears correct:

validate.js

*The function **send_if_valid()** is called from the HTML **onclick** attribute of the button in this example.*

```javascript
// a function to validate an email address
function send_if_valid()
{
  if( document.forms.f.email.value.indexOf("@")== -1 )
  fail("No '@' in address");
  else
  {
    var adr = document.forms.f.email.value.split("@");
    if(adr[0].length < 1 ) fail("User address absent");
    else if(adr[1].indexOf(".")== -1) fail("No dot");
    else if(adr[1].length < 3) fail("Domain incorrect");
    else document.forms.f.submit();
  }
}

// a function to display an error message
function fail(msg)
{ alert("Email Address Error:\n" +msg); }
```

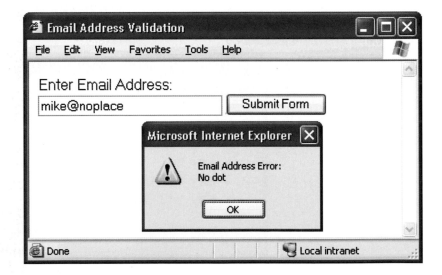

Event-handlers

User actions, such as a key depression or a mouse click, create events that JavaScript can use to interact with the user. This chapter describes common events and illustrates how they may be used by a JavaScript event-handler.

Covers

Chapter Twelve

Mouse click

The most common interactive event is the **Click** event created when a user clicks the left-hand mouse button while the cursor is over a form button in a Web document.

An **onclick** event-handler is normally assigned in the button's HTML **<input>** tag with the HTML **onclick** attribute.

Put single quotes inside the double quotes used to assign a string.

Typically the value assigned to the **onclick** attribute will be a call to a JavaScript function that will execute statements. For instance...

```
<input type="button" value="Do Click"
onclick="do_click('JavaScript in easy steps')"/>
```

This simple example calls a JavaScript function when the user clicks on a button and passes a string argument for use by the called function:

click.js

```
// a function to react to the CLICK event
function do_click( str )
{
  // display the passed string argument
  alert(str);
}
```

Capture mouse

It is extremely useful to know the whereabouts of the cursor when dealing with JavaScript in DHTML scripting.

Whenever the user moves the cursor a **MouseMove** event occurs and this can be captured by JavaScript for use with an **onmousemove** event-handler.

The first script statement in this example is to trap mouse movements in Netscape – capitalization must be exactly correct.

The example below gives a useful way of determining x,y screen coordinates when developing DHTML scripts.

The **MouseMove** event is captured, then the **onmousemove** event-handler dynamically displays the cursor's x,y coordinates in a form text field named **txt**:

mousemove.html

```
// Netscape/Mozilla capture events instruction
if(navigator.appName == "Netscape")
window.captureEvents(Event.MOUSEMOVE);

// a function to react to the MOUSEMOVE event
function track(e)
{
  var x = (document.all) ? event.x : e.pageX;
  var y = (document.all) ? event.y : e.pageY;
  document.forms.f.txt.value = "X: " +x+ "  Y: " +y;
}

// specify the onmousemove event-handler
document.onmousemove=track;
```

*The **document.all** property is found in Internet Explorer but not Netscape/Mozilla browsers – it can be useful to apply browser-specific code.*

The Netscape and Internet Explorer DOM use different object names for the cursor's x,y position.

MouseMove Event
File   Edit   View   Favorites   Tools   Help
X: 200 Y: 60
Done   Local intranet

Mouse over

A **MouseOver** event occurs when the user places the cursor over a object on a Web page.

The anchor **\<a\>** element can specify an event-handler for the **MouseOver** event by assigning a JavaScript function call to the HTML **onmouseover** attribute, like this:

```
<a href = "target.html" onmouseover = "do_mouseover()"/>
```

Most frequently the event-handler will perform an image swap as a rollover effect but any statements may be executed.

The example below assigns a string value to an input text box when the cursor is placed over an image:

mouseover.js

```
// a function to react to the MOUSEOVER event
function do_mouseover()
{
  // display a message in a form field
  document.forms.f.txt.value = "Mouse is Over the link";
}
```

Mouse out

A **MouseOut** event occurs when the user moves the cursor away from a HTML hyperlink on a Web page.

The anchor **<a>** element can specify an event-handler for the **MouseOut** event by assigning a JavaScript function call to the HTML **onmouseout** attribute, like this:

```
<a href = "target.html" onmouseout="do_mouseout()"
onmouseover = "do_mouseover()"/>
```

Most frequently the event-handler will perform an image swap to return an image to its original state in a rollover.

The following example builds on the previous example by adding an **onmouseout** event-handler to change the value of a text box when the cursor moves off the link:

mouseout.js

```
// a function to react to the MOUSEOUT event
function do_mouseout()
{
  document.forms.f.txt.value = "Mouse is Off the link";
}

// a function to react to the MOUSEOVER event
function do_mouseover()
{
  document.forms.f.txt.value = "Mouse is Over the link";
}
```

This illustration shows the text field after the cursor has moved over the image.

Mouse down and mouse up

A **MouseDown** event occurs when the user presses a mouse button and a **MouseUp** event occurs when it is released.

Typically these are used together so that a single mouse click will use two event-handlers, like this:

```
<input type = "button" value = "Light Switch"
onmousedown = "light(1)" onmouseup = "light(0)"/>
```

This example swaps an image and changes the value of a text box when the cursor is over the image and a mouse button is pressed. It reverts both to their original state when the button is released:

mouse-updown.js

*The document, link, image and button HTML elements all support attributes for **onmouseup** and **onmousedown**.*

```
// a function to react to MOUSEDOWN and MOUSEUP events
function light(n)
{
  if( n == 1 )
  {
    document.images.bulb.src = "bulbon.gif";
    document.forms.f.txt.value = "Button is Down";
  }
  if( n == 0 )
  {
    document.images.bulb.src = "bulboff.gif";
    document.forms.f.txt.value = "Button is Up";
  }
}
```

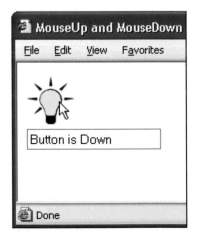

Mouse buttons

JavaScript can determine which mouse button has been pressed by examining properties of the **MouseDown** event.

With Internet Explorer the left mouse button stores an integer value of 1 in the **event.button** property, the right mouse button stores an integer value of 2 and the center button, if present, stores an integer value of 3.

Here this property is used to inhibit the Internet Explorer context menu that normally appears when the right mouse button is pressed by the user:

mouse-button.js

```javascript
// store a default message
var msg = "Right-Click Context Menu Is Disabled";

// a function to stop the IE context menu
function stopmenu(e)
{
  // for Internet Explorer browsers
  if(navigator.appName == "Microsoft Internet Explorer"
  && ( event.button == 2 || event.button == 3 ))
  {
    alert( msg );
    return false;
  }                                         }

// specify the onmousedown event-handler
document.onmousedown = stopmenu;
```

Key down and key up

A **KeyDown** event occurs when the user presses a keyboard key button and a **KeyUp** event occurs when it is released. Typically these are used together so that a single key depression will use two event-handlers.

This example swaps an image and changes the value of a text box when a keyboard key button is pressed but reverts both to their original state when the key button is released:

key-updown.js

```
// Netscape/Mozilla capture events instruction
if( navigator.appName == "Netscape" )
window.captureEvents( Event.KEYDOWN, Event.KEYUP );

// a function to react to KEYDOWN events
function isdown()
{
  document.images.bulb.src = "bulbon.gif";
  document.forms.f.txt.value = "Key is Down";
}

// a function to react to KEYUP events
function isup()
{
  document.images.bulb.src = "bulboff.gif";
  document.forms.f.txt.value = "Key is Up";
}

// define the event-handlers
document.onkeydown = isdown;
document.onkeyup = isup;
```

Notice how the first two lines of this script capture both KeyDown and KeyUp events for Netscape/Mozilla browsers.

KeyUp and KeyDown	KeyUp and KeyDown
File Edit View Favorites	File Edit View Favorites
Key is Down	Key is Up
Done	Done

Key codes

The **KeyDown** event can also be used to get the Unicode character code number of a key depression.

This example looks for the Y and N character codes, in both upper and lower case, then branches the script according to the value.

key-codes.js

```
// Netscape/Mozilla capture events instruction
  if( navigator.appName == "Netscape")
window.captureEvents( Event.KEYDOWN );

function showkey(e)
{
  var msg = "", fwd = "Y pressed", hlt = "N pressed";

  // check key codes in Netscape/Mozilla browsers
  if( navigator.appName == "Netscape" )
  {
    if( e.which == 89 || e.which == 121 ) msg = fwd;
    if( e.which == 78 || e.which == 110)  msg = hlt;
  }

  // check key codes in Internet Explorer
  if(navigator.appName == "Microsoft Internet Explorer")
  {
    if(event.keyCode==89 || event.keyCode==121)msg= fwd;
    if(event.keyCode==78 || event.keyCode==110)msg= hlt;
  }

  // display the appropriate message
  if( msg != "" ) alert(msg);
}

// define the event-handler
document.onkeydown=showkey;
```

Unicode values for common characters are the same as ASCII codes so in this example Y=89, N=78 y=121 and n=110.

[JavaScript Application]

⚠ Y pressed

OK

Load

The **Load** event does not occur until all the HTML elements on a Web page have completely loaded. This means that the **onload** event-handler will only run after all the elements are present.

If JavaScript is to modify elements of the document **<body>** section those elements must already be loaded to avoid receiving a script error.

Typically the **onload** event-handler will call a JavaScript function, often named **init()**, that will initialize a number of values.

This example sets the HTML page colors, then it assigns a value to a variable which it subsequently assigns to a form text box:

load.js

```javascript
// a function to react to the LOAD event
function init()
{
  // set foreground and background colors
  document.bgColor = "orange";
  document.fgColor = "blue";

  // store a string then display it in a form field
  var str = "The Page is Loaded";
  document.forms.f.txt.value = str;
}

// specify the onload event-handler
window.onload = init;
```

*A HTML event-handler assigned to the **onload** attribute of the **<body>** tag would replace that assigned in the script.*

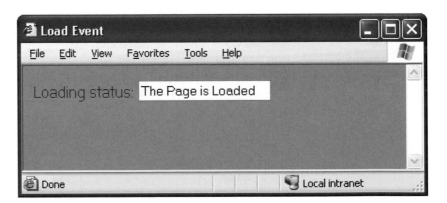

Unload

The **Unload** event occurs whenever the browser unloads a document from a window, or frame, usually when the user navigates to a new URL.

The **onunload** event-handler may call a final JavaScript function to be run just before the document unloads. When a frames page is unloaded the **onunload** event-handler of each frame may call a final function.

The **onunload** event-handler is useful to save the final state of data on that page in a cookie or by submission to the server.

It is also used to open new pop-up windows containing further information that the user may find useful.

The example below illustrates the use of the **onunload** event-handler to open a new pop-up window:

unload.js

```
// a function to react to the ONUNLOAD event
function leaving()
{
  // open a HTML document in a pop-up window
  var win = window.open("finally.html", "",
  "top=50,left-50,width=300,height=100" );
}

// specify the onunload event-handler
window.onunload - leaving;
```

*The **onunload** event-handler can also be assigned to the HTML **onunload** attribute in the **<body>** tag – care should be taken not to overwrite event-handlers.*

Focus

The **Focus** event occurs when the user clicks on a form element or on a window to direct the browser's focus.

The **onfocus** event-handler can call a JavaScript function when the focus is received.

A HTML **onfocus** attribute can be added to form elements to specify a function to execute when it receives focus, like this...

*Notice how the JavaScript **this** keyword is used to pass the object references* document.forms.f.txt1 *and* document.forms.f.txt2.

```
<input type="text" name="txt1"
   value="Enter quantity here" onfocus="wipe(this)"/>
<input type="text" name="txt2"
   value="Enter data here" onfocus="wipe(this)"/>
```

In the example below, the text inputs initially display the strings assigned to their respective **value** attributes.

When the user clicks either text input it receives focus so the **wipe()** function assigns an empty string to its **value** attribute. This clears the displayed text and places the cursor in the appropriate position ready for the user to input text into that field.

focus.js

```
// a function to clear a text input
function wipe( obj )
{
  // clear the form field
  obj.value="";
  //  reset the focus
  obj.focus();
}
```

The intrinsic JavaScript isNaN() *function can be used to check if a value is Not a Number.*

Focus Event

File   Edit   View   Favorites   Tools   Help

Quantity: [   ]
Description: [Enter data here   ]

Done   Local intranet

Blur

A **Blur** event occurs when the browser's focus moves away from a form element, or a window, and the **onblur** event-handler may then call a JavaScript function.

The **blur()** method of a form element is useful to prevent user input for text boxes that must be read-only.

A **blur()** method can be called from the HTML **onfocus** attribute of the read-only element, like this...

```
<input type="text" size="30"
 value="This field is read-only" onfocus="blur(this)"/>
```

In the following example the user is reminded that the text box they have just left should receive some input:

blur.js

```
// a function to examine a passed string argument
function is_entry( val )
{
  // if the text field is empty
  if ( val == "" )
  // ...display a message
  alert( "Please enter data" );

}
```

Using the window.blur() method will typically minimize the window.

Change

The **Change** event occurs when the value of a text input is changed or when the user selects an item in an options list.

The **onchange** event-handler can call a JavaScript function to execute some code whenever the **Change** event occurs.

The example below sets the initial selected option to **Green** then assigns an event-handler that displays the associated value in a text box whenever the selection is changed:

change.js

```
// a function to set the selected item in a list
function init()
{
  document.forms.f.s.options[1].selected = true;
  // specify an onchange event-handler
  document.forms.f.s.onchange = show_selected;
}
```

This example relates to a `<select>` element with the id of `s` in a `<form>` with the id of `f`.

```
// a function to display the selected list item
function show_selected()
{
  document.forms.f.txt.value =
 document.forms.f.s.options[document.forms.f.s.selectedIndex].value;
}

// specify the onload event-handler
window.onload = init;
```

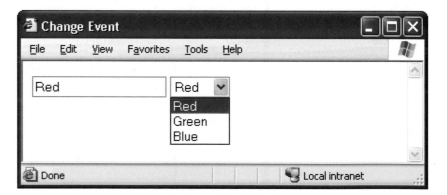

Reset

The **Reset** event occurs when the user pushes a form's reset button or when JavaScript executes the **form.reset()** method.

The **onreset** event-handler may call a JavaScript function when the **Reset** event occurs.

In this example there are two HTML forms , named **f1** and **f2**. The first form contains three radio buttons and a reset button. An event-handler is assigned to the HTML **onreset** attribute in the first **<form>** tag. When the reset button is pressed the value of the second radio button is changed and its value is displayed in a text box in the second form.

reset.js

```
// a function to set the value of a radio button
function show_value()
{
  // set the value
  document.forms.f1.r[0].value = "Salmon";
  // display the set value
  document.forms.f2.txt.value =
    document.forms.f1.r[0].value;
}
```

*The first radio button could be checked with JavaScript by assigning **true** to the property **document.forms.f1.r[0].checked**.*

Submit

The **Submit** event occurs when the user pushes a submit button in a form. The **onsubmit** event-handler may call a function to carry out form validation before submission.

If the **onsubmit** event-handler returns **false**, for instance when form validation fails, the form data will not be sent.

This example performs basic email address validation and provides the user with an **alert()** message if validation fails. The function is called by the HTML **onsubmit** attribute of the **<form>** tag.

submit.js

```
// a function to validate basic email address format
function validation()
{
  // seek an @ character in the address
  if(document.forms.f.email.value.indexOf( "@" ) == -1)
  {
    // if absent display a message
    alert( "Email address is absent or incorrect" );
    // ...and do not submit the form
    return false;
  }
}
```

The onsubmit event-handler is not invoked by use of the form.submit() method in JavaScript.

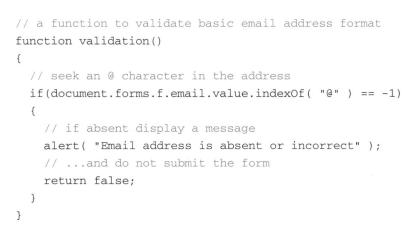

Abort

Internet Explorer allows an event-handler to be specified for the **Abort** event that occurs when the user cancels the download of an image – usually by pushing the **stop** button on the browser's toolbar. The **onabort** event-handler may call a JavaScript function when an image download is cancelled.

To identify the image a name must be given to its **id** attribute in the HTML **<img>** element, like this...

```
<img id="big-pic" src="bigpic.jpg" alt=""/>
```

An event-handler can then be assigned to that image's **onabort** property. In the example below the event-handler directly creates an **alert()** message confirming that the download is cancelled:

abort.js

```
// for Internet Explorer only set an abort event-handler
if(document.all)
document.getElementById("big-pic").onabort = abort_msg;

// a function to display a confirmation message
function abort_msg()
{
    alert( "Image Download Has Been Aborted" );
}
```

The <script> element that includes this script must appear in the HTML document body after the <img> element – an event-handler can't be set until the image object exists.

This feature is useful to switch the image source to a low-resolution version.

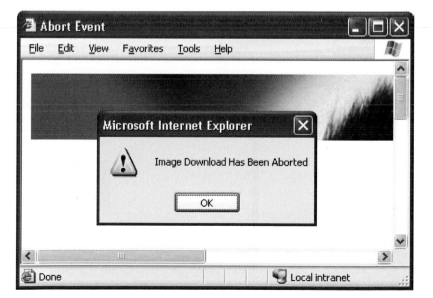

Resize

The **Resize** event occurs when a browser window is re-sized by the user and the **onresize** event-handler can execute a function to make the page appropriate for the new window size.

This is most useful to reposition DHTML page components as illustrated in the following example. This creates a centered **<div>** element with the **id** of **lyr** which will be re-centered when the window is re-sized:

resize.js

```
// a function to center a <div> element
function set_pos()
{
  var width;
  // get the window width
  if(navigator.appName == "Netscape")
  width = innerWidth;                // for Netscape/Mozilla
  else
  width = document.body.clientWidth;          // for IE

  // half window width minus half div width
  var left_pos = parseInt((width / 2) -50);

  // set the left position of the <div> element
 document.getElementById("lyr").style.left=(left_pos+"px");
}

// specify the onresize event-handler
window.onresize=set_pos;
```

HOT TIP

*This **<div>** is initially centered by calling the **set_pos()** function from the **onload** attribute of the HTML **<body>** element.*

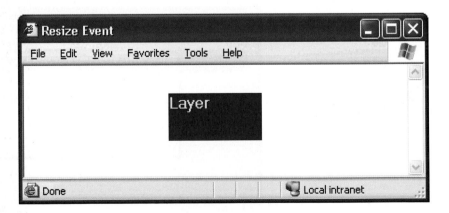

JavaScript in DHTML

This chapter describes the use of JavaScript to control and manipulate components of a HTML document. The many examples illustrate how characteristics of position, content and visibility can all be dynamically changed to create an exciting interactive Web page.

Covers

Chapter Thirteen

JavaScript: protocol

The **javascript:** protocol may be assigned to the **href** attribute in a HTML **<a>** anchor element to make a JavaScript function the target of a hyperlink.

The name of the function should follow the protocol specifier to identify the script code to be executed, or short pieces of code can be included in-line after the specifier, like this:

```
<a href="javascript:alert('In-line code')">Link #1</a>
<a href="javascript:respond()">Link #2</a>
```

This example contains both in-line code and a function call. Each will execute when the user clicks the relevant hyperlink:

protocol.js

```
// a function to display a simple message
function respond()
{
    alert("JavaScript code");
}
```

*To make an anchor that has no target use **javascript://** so that other attributes like **onmouseover** can still be used.*

![JavaScript: Protocol browser window showing Link #1 Link #2 and a Microsoft Internet Explorer alert dialog displaying "In-line code" with an OK button. Status bar shows javascript:alert('In-line code') and Local intranet.]

Layer attributes

Probably the most important **style** attributes of a **<div>** element to be used in DHTML are **id, top, left, z-index, visibility, color** and **background-color**.

These **style** attributes can be dynamically changed by assigning new values to them with JavaScript.

This example demonstrates how to access each of these attributes by listing the values of a **<div>** element called **lyr**:

layer.js

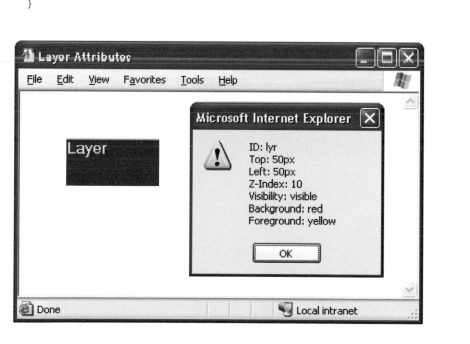

The CSS **z-index** style is referenced in JavaScript by the term **zIndex**. Also the CSS **background-color** style is referenced in JavaScript by the term **backgroundColor**.

```javascript
// a function to display the style attributes of a <div>
function get_styles()
{
  var obj = document.getElementById("lyr");
  var str = "ID: " + obj.id;
  str += "\nTop: " + obj.style.top;
  str += "\nLeft: " + obj.style.left;
  str += "\nZ-Index: " + obj.style.zIndex;
  str += "\nVisibility: " + obj.style.visibility;
  str += "\nBackground: " + obj.style.backgroundColor;
  str += "\nForeground: " + obj.style.color;
  alert(str);
}
```

Toggle visibility

Having determined how to access layer styles with JavaScript it's easy to have some fun with them by letting the JavaScript code dynamically change their values.

For example, changing the **visibility** style value to **hidden** will cause a layer to disappear from view.

Conversely a layer initially created with a **visibility** style value of **hidden** can be revealed by changing that value to **visible**.

The following script toggles the **visibility** of a single layer with **onmouseover** and **onmouseout** event-handlers, like this:

```
<a href="javascript://" onmouseover="show_apple()"
onmouseout="hide_apple()">Apple Link</a>
```

This script could easily toggle several layers for even greater effect:

visibility.js

```
// a function to reveal a layer
function show_apple()
{
  // reference the layer by id
  var obj = getElementById("lyr");
  // show the layer
  obj.style.visibility= "visible";
}

// a function to hide a layer
function hide_apple()
{
  // reference the layer by id
  var obj = getElementById("lyr");
  // hide the layer
  obj.style.visibility= "hidden";
}
```

The illustrations on the opposite page demonstrate the effect of this script when the user places the cursor over, and off, the hyperlink.

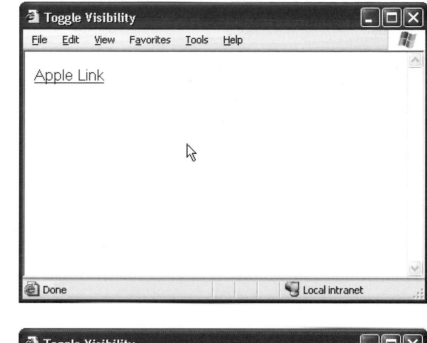

The *javascript:* protocol specifier will appear in the status bar in place of a target url address.

Dynamic content

JavaScript can write content onto a layer without affecting the contents elsewhere on the page.

Although this example uses text from user input JavaScript could write layer content from any function call.

The position of the layer will remain unaltered but the height of the layer will be automatically increased if the content will not fit into the existing layer size.

Also text will automatically wrap intelligently at the layer border so words will not be split.

The JavaScript example for this feature will create a layer, then dynamically write the user-entered text onto the layer when the user pushes the input button.

write-layer.js

```
// create a <div> layer
document.write("<div id='lyr' style='position:absolute;
top:90px;left:10px;width:200px;height:10px;z-index:10;
background-color:orange'> </div>");

// a function to write a user-entered string on a layer
function write_entry()
{
  // get the string entry
  var str = document.forms.f.txt.value;

  // reference the layer by id
  var obj = document.getElementById("lyr");

  // open the layer document
  obj.document.open();

  // write the string
  obj.document.write(str);

  // close the layer document
  obj.document.close();
}
```

*Insert the **<script>** element to include JavaScripts that write layers within the body section of the HTML document.*

The illustrations on the facing page demonstrate the effect of this script when the user enters a string into the text field then clicks the push button.

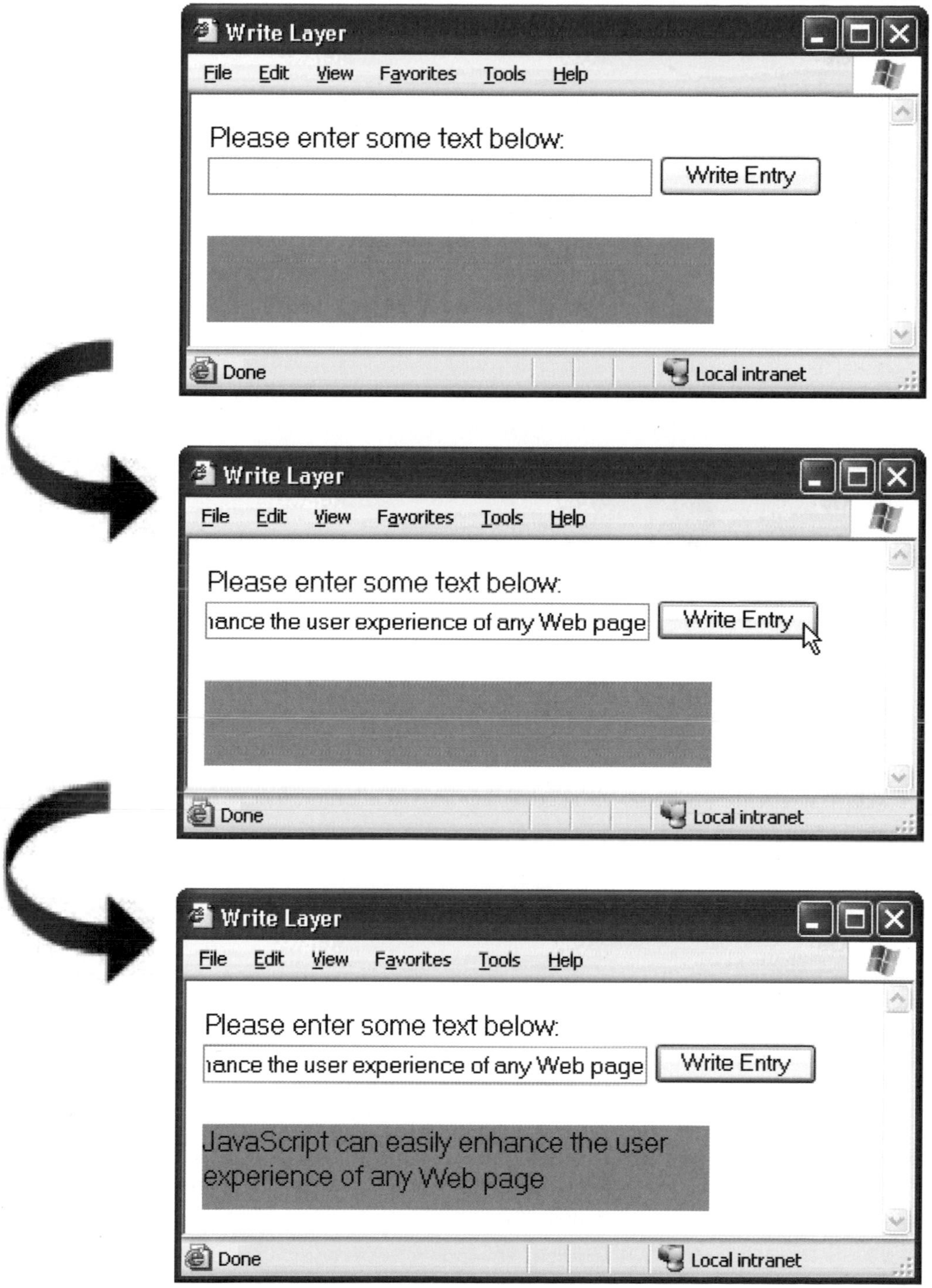
Write Layer
File Edit View Favorites Tools Help
Please enter some text below:
Write Entry
Done
Local intranet
Write Layer
File Edit View Favorites Tools Help
Please enter some text below:
ance the user experience of any Web page
Write Entry
Done
Local intranet
Write Layer
File Edit View Favorites Tools Help
Please enter some text below:
ance the user experience of any Web page
Write Entry
JavaScript can easily enhance the user experience of any Web page
Done
Local intranet

Slide show

JavaScript can rotate images to create an automatic slide show that will update the current image after a predetermined interval.

In this script a preload routine first downloads all the images into the browser's cache to be readily available for display.

Rotation speed in milliseconds is specified by the value assigned to the variable named **pause**.

The variable named **n** is a counter that is incremented by the **rotate()** timer function and is used to display the image at that index number in the **imgs[]** array.

It is important that all the images should have the same dimensions and be small file sizes to avoid download delays.

slide-show.js

```
// store an interval in a variable
var pause = 3000;
// create and initialize a counter
var n = 0;
// create an array of image file names
var imgs = new Array ( "butterfly.gif", "globe.gif",
"fish.gif", "clock.gif" );

// preload all the images
var preload = new Array();
for( var i = 1; i < imgs.length; i++ )
{
  preload[i] = new Image();
  preload[i].src = imgs[i];
}
```

*Simply adding more image filenames to the **imgs[]** array will extend the slide show without further coding.*

```
// a function to display each image for the set interval
function rotate()
{
  document.images.pic.src = imgs[n];
  ( n == (imgs.length - 1 )) ? n = 0 : n++;
  setTimeout( "rotate()", pause );
}

// specify the onload event-handler
window.onload = rotate;
```

The HTML code used with the JavaScript slide show assigns the name **pic** to the original image – so the script may address the image object as **document.images.pic**:

```html
<img name="pic" src="butterfly.gif" width="150"
   height="150" alt=""/>
```

Ensure that all images are the actual size to be displayed so that the browser does not need to re-size them when displaying.

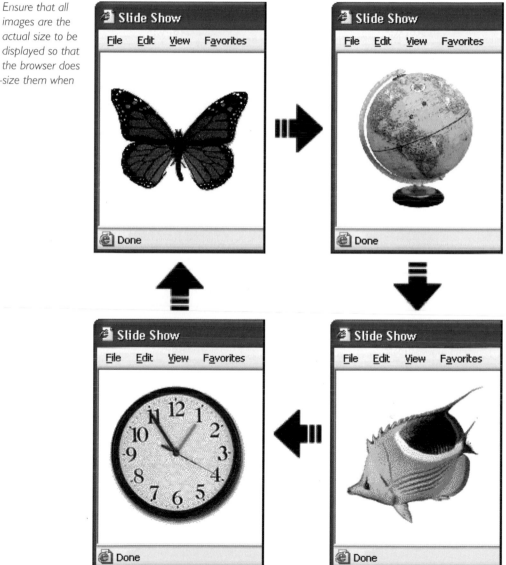

Tacking layer

The **left** coordinate of a layer object's **style** can be modified by JavaScript to reposition the layer along the X axis.

The following example moves a **<div>** layer that has an **id** of **boat**. This contains a sailboat image just outside the left edge of the window. A timer function sails the boat across the screen.

When the boat disappears off the right edge of the window JavaScript swaps the image for a pre-loaded version of the sailboat image facing in the opposite direction. The script then sails it back across the screen from right to left.

When the boat disappears off the left edge of the window the image reverts to the original version that proceeds to sail left to right and the boat continues to tack back and forth.

The **go_right** variable determines the direction of travel. It's initially set to **true** but it is reversed at each extreme point.

The **ext** variable stores the width of the window according to the type of browser running the script.

The **set_sail()** function is initially called from the script to start the routine then is called recursively from inside the function itself.

Use an animated GIF image with this script to create even more exciting results.

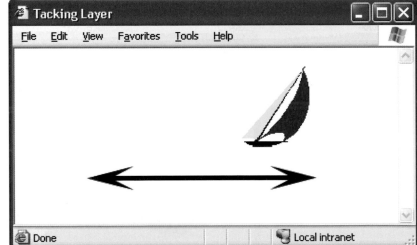

tack.js

This script must be included in the `<body>` section of the HTML document – after the `<div>` element is created.

```javascript
// preload the swap image
var preload = new Image(); preload.src = "sail_l.gif";
// set the initial direction to right
var go_right = true;

// a function to move a <div> across the page
function set_sail()
{
  // get the div object
  var obj = document.getElementById("boat");

  // get the window width
  var ext;
  if(document.body.clientWidth) ext =
    document.body.clientWidth;
  if(window.innerWidth) ext = window.innerWidth;

  // move by 1 pixel in set direction
  if(go_right )
  obj.style.left = (parseInt(obj.style.left)+1)+"px";
  else
  obj.style.left = (parseInt(obj.style.left)-1)+"px";

  // change direction at the right extreme
  if(parseInt(obj.style.left ) >= ( ext + 5 ) )
  {
    go_right=false;
    document.images.boat_image.src = "sail_l.gif";
  }

  // change direction at the left extreme
  if(parseInt(obj.style.left) <= -75)
  {
    go_right = true;
    document.boat_image.src = "sail_r.gif";
  }

  // set the interval to call this function
  window.setTimeout("set_sail()", 50);
}

// start the routine
set_sail();
```

The positional pixel values have "px" tacked on the end (e.g.: left="70px") so the __parseInt()__ method is needed to extract the integer part for manipulation.

Scrolling layer

Where the previous example modified the **left** property of a layer object's **style**, this example manipulates the layer's **top** property to move a layer higher or lower on the Y axis.

This example moves a **<div>** layer that has an **id** of **chopper**. The layer contains a simple helicopter image.

HTML code adds rollover hyperlinks that call JavaScript functions but have a **void** target.

When the user places the cursor over the hyperlink "Soar" a timer function increments the value of the top property so the layer moves vertically higher in the window.

Placing the cursor over the hyperlink "Sink" has the opposite effect and lowers the layer vertically in the window.

In each case the timer function is cancelled when the cursor moves away from the hyperlink and the movement of the layer is discontinued.

Keeping the cursor over the "Soar" link will cause the image to go off the top of the window. A conditional limiter could be added to prevent this.

scroll.js

```
// a variable to store a timer
var timer;

// a function to move a <div> layer up the page
function soar()
{
  // get the div object
  var obj = document.getElementById("chopper");

  // move up by 1 pixel
  obj.style.top = (parseInt(obj.style.top)-1)+"px";

  // set the interval at which to call this function
  timer = window.setTimeout("soar()", 50);
}

// a function to move a <div> layer down the page
function sink()
{
  // get the div object
  var obj = document.getElementById("chopper");

  // move down by 1 pixel
  obj.style.top = (parseInt(obj.style.top)+1)+"px";

  // set the interval at which to call this function
  timer = window.setTimeout("sink()", 50);
}

// a function to cancel the timer
function stop()
{
  clearTimeout(timer);
}
```

*The **parseInt()** method is needed to extract the layer's top value.*

Change the timer delay from 50 to adjust the speed of scroll.

And the HTML code for the rollovers looks like this:

```
<a href = "javascript://" onmouseover = "soar()"
onmouseout = "stop()">Soar</a>

<a href = "javascript://" onmouseover = "sink()"
onmouseout = "stop()">Sink</a>
```

Pop-up layers

This example builds on the earlier visibility toggle script by using multiple layers which have their visibility toggled by an image map.

When the cursor is placed over an image map hyperlink, the JavaScript function will display the appropriate layer but will hide that layer when the cursor moves off the link.

Both layers are created in the HTML code with their **visibility** style property set to **hidden** – so they are not initially visible. Placing the cursor over an active area of the image causes the **onmouseover** event to call the **talk()** function. The function call passes a string argument to identify which active area is the caller. This determines which layer object is to be manipulated.

The **talk()** function sets the **visibility** style of the appropriate layer object to **visible** – so it becomes visible. Moving the cursor off an active area causes the **onmouseout** event to call the **hush()** function, again passing a string argument identifier. This once more sets the **visibility** style of the appropriate layer object to **hidden** – so it becomes invisible again.

This type of dynamic script can be used to great effect with navigation menu item rollovers.

popup-layers.js

Make the layers'
z-index values
different if the
layers overlap.

```javascript
// a function to toggle visibility on
function talk(str)
{
  // a variable to store the object
  var obj;

  // get the appropriate div layer
  if(str == "sal") obj = document.getElementById("sal");
  if(str == "har") obj = document.getElementById("har");

  // show the layer
  obj.style.visibility = "visible";
}

// a function to toggle visibility off
function hush(str)
{
  // a variable to store the object
  var obj;

  // get the appropriate div layer
  if(str == "sal") obj = document.getElementById("sal");
  if(str == "har") obj = document.getElementById("har");

  // hide the layer
  obj.style.visibility = "hidden";
}
```

And the HTML code for the image map looks like this:

Avoid creating
adjacent active
areas – always
leave a small gap
to allow time for
onmouseout events to fire
before starting another
onmouseover event. The areas
in this example cover the faces
of the people in the image.

```html
<img src="couple.jpg" usemap="#couple" alt=""/>
<map id="couple" name="couple">

<area shape="rect" href="javascript://" alt=""
coords="41,26,138,143"
onmouseover="talk('sal')" onmouseout="hush('sal')"/>

<area shape="poly" href="javascript://" alt=""
coords="244,69,208,132,202,185,227,205,298,171,318,110,247,65"
onmouseover="talk('har')" onmouseout="hush('har')"/>

</map>
```

Dynamic menu

This example uses the mouse coordinates to toggle the visibility of menu layers and uses a stylesheet to specify the characteristics of the main bar layer and the menu layers:

menus.js

Remember to capture the MouseMove event for Netscape users.

Different width of menu heading and menu item descriptions will require changes to the boundary coordinates used in this example.

```javascript
// Netscape/Mozilla capture events instruction
if(navigator.appName == "Netscape")
  window.captureEvents(Event.MOUSEMOVE);

// specify the onmousemove event-handler
document.onmousemove = track;

// get the menu layer objects
var m1 = document.getElementById("menu_1");
var m2 = document.getElementById("menu_2");
var m3 = document.getElementById("menu_3");

// a function to react to the MOUSEMOVE event
// and to dynamically hide menu layers
function track(e)
{
  // get the current x,y coordinates
  var x = (document.all) ? event.x : e.pageX;
  var y = (document.all) ? event.y : e.pageY;

  // hide menu 1 if out of bounds
  if( x<1 || x>60 || y<53 || y>123)
   m1.style.visibility = "hidden";
  // hide menu 2 if out of bounds
  if( x<70 || x>130 || y<53 || y>123)
   m2.style.visibility = "hidden";
  // hide menu 3 if out of bounds
  if( x<140 || x>200 || y<53 || y>123)
   m3.style.visibility = "hidden";
}

// a function to reveal a menu layer
function reveal(menu)
{
  if(menu == 1) m1.style.visibility = "visible";
  if(menu == 2) m2.style.visibility = "visible";
  if(menu == 3) m3.style.visibility = "visible";
}
```

The HTML code for the bar and one menu looks like this...

menus.html
(part of)

```
<div id="bar">
<a href="javascript://" onmouseover="reveal(1)">
   Menu 1</a> |
<a href="javascript://" onmouseover="reveal(2)">
   Menu 2</a> |
<a href="javascript://" onmouseover="reveal(3)">
   Menu 3</a>
</div>
```

The **menu_2** layer has a style **left** value of **70px** and the **menu_3** layer has a style **left** value of **140px**.

```
<div id="menu_1" class="menu" style="left:0px">
<a href="target1.html"> Item 1 </a><br/>
<a href="target2.html"> Item 2 </a><br/>
<a href="target3.html"> Item 3 </a>
</div>
```

and the CSS rules for the bar and menus look like this...

menus.css
(part of)

```
#bar { position:absolute; left:0px; top:50px;
color:black; width:800px; height:20px;
background-color:#FFC0CB; font-family:verdana; font-
size:10pt; border-color:white; border-width:1px }

.menu { position:absolute; width:60px; height:50px;
background-color:#FFC0CB; top:71px; visibility:hidden;
font-family:verdana; font-size:10pt;
border-color:white; border-width:1px }
```

Both stylesheet rules fix the font height – this prevents changes in the browser font settings from disrupting the layer sizes.

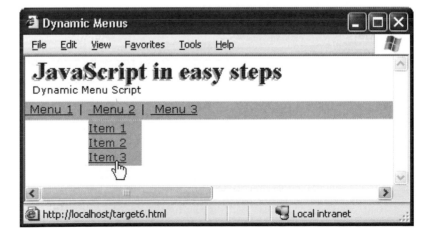

Fresh options

In this example JavaScript dynamically changes menu options and their associated values depending on which radio button is checked. The HTML **<select>** element in this example has the **id** of **city** and includes four **<option>** elements.

dynamic-list.js
(part of)

```
// a function to determine which radio button is checked
function set_cities(n)
{
  if(document.forms.f.rad[0].checked) jap();
  if(document.forms.f.rad[1].checked) usa();
}

// a function to display the selected list option
function show_value()
{
document.forms.f.txt.value =
  document.forms.f.city.options
    [document.forms.f.city.selectedIndex].value;
}

// a function to assign US city options
function usa()
{
  // set option 0
  with(document.forms.f.city.options[0])
  {
    selected = true;
    text = "Select City...";
    value="";
  }
  // set option 1
  with(document.forms.f.city.options[1])
  { text="New York"; value="new york"; }

  // set option 2
  with(document.forms.f.city.options[2])
  { text="Los Angeles"; value="los angeles"; }

  // set option 3
  with(document.forms.f.city.options[3])
  { text="Washington"; value="washington"; }
}
```

*The value of the **selected** option is displayed in the text box – just for demonstration purposes.*

dynamic-list.js (cont'd)

*JavaScript can only manipulate **<option>** elements that exist in the HTML code – it cannot create new options.*

```javascript
// a function to assign Japanese city options
function jap()
{
  // set option 0
  with(document.forms.f.city.options[0])
  {
    selected = true;
    text = "Select City...";
    value="";
  }

  // set option 1
  with(document.forms.f.city.options[1])
  { text="Kyoto"; value="kyoto"; }

  // set option 2
  with(document.forms.f.city.options[2])
  { text="Osaka"; value="osaka"; }

  // set option 3
  with(document.forms.f.city.options[3])
  { text="Tokyo"; value="tokyo"; }
}
```

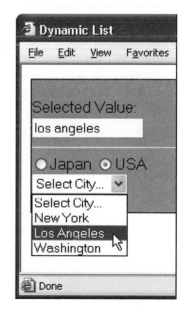

DOM reference

The chart below illustrates the important parts of the Document Object Model (DOM) to explain how the objects in a Web page are related. Those marked with an ★ are specific to Microsoft Internet Explorer and are not found in other browsers.

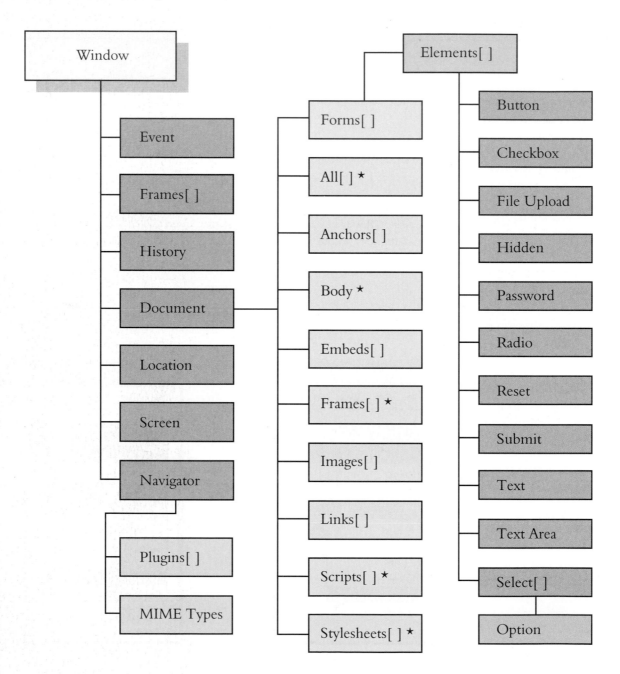

JavaScript in e-commerce

This final chapter shows how some of the earlier examples may be applied to e-commerce applications and illustrates how frames can store data for later use in other frames.

Covers

Chapter Fourteen

The products page

The example in this chapter follows the development of an on-line order that starts with a page from which the user may select quantities of items to order.

The page is framed with a left-hand panel named **menu** and a right-hand larger frame named **main**.

*The frames must be named with the **name** attribute of the **<frame>** tags in the frameholder document.*

Typically the **menu** frame will remain constantly displayed while the **main** frame will display different pages as the user navigates around the site.

A button is added at the bottom of the form that will advance the user to the next stage of the order process.

In the form, depicted below, the user has entered quantity requirement for some of the illustrated products:

Enhance this page with the addition of pop-up windows over each image giving fuller product details for that item.

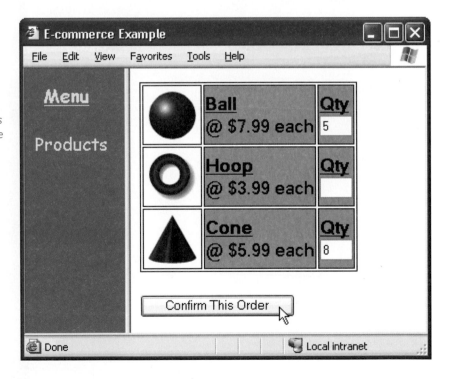

The frame-holder document for this example is named **e-commerce.html**. It displays a **menu.html** in the **menu** frame and (initially) **products.html** in the **main** frame – as shown above.

A hidden form

The page in the menu frame contains a hidden form named **m** (for memory) that will retain the order data while the pages in the main frame are changed.

*The text inputs on the product page are named **ball**, **hoop** and **cone**.*

It consists of input items that mirror those of the form named **f** on the product page together with inputs for customer name, account number and order number.

*menu.html
(part of)*

```html
<!-- a form to store order data -->

<form id = "m" action = "" method = "post">

<input type = "hidden" name = "customer" value = ""/>
<input type = "hidden" name = "accountnum" value = ""/>
<input type = "hidden" name = "ordernum" value = ""/>
<input type = "hidden" name = "ball" value = ""/>
<input type = "hidden" name = "hoop" value = ""/>
<input type = "hidden" name = "cone" value = ""/>

</form>
```

The **onclick** attribute of the button on the products page calls a JavaScript function that fills the values of the hidden form **m** with the values entered by the user into the products page form **f**. It then loads a new page into the **main** frame.

products.js

```javascript
// a function to store values in a form in another frame
function populate()
{
  // variables for the form objects
  var m = parent.frames.menu.document.forms.m;
  var f = document.forms.f;

  // copy the values
  m.ball.value = f.ball.value;
  m.hoop.value = f.hoop.value;
  m.cone.value = f.cone.value;

  //load a new page into this frame
  window.location = "customer.html";
}
```

Get the customer details

The next page in the **main** frame, **customer.html**, requests the customer's name and account number.

When the user clicks the button on this page its **onclick** attribute calls a JavaScript function to store the user input. This copies the values of the form **f** inputs on this page to the identically-named hidden inputs in the memory form **m** in the **menu** frame.

customer.js

```javascript
// a function to store values in a form in another frame
function populate()
{
  // variables for the form objects
  var m = parent.frames.menu.document.forms.m;
  var f = document.forms.f;

  // copy the values
  m.customer.value = f.customer.value;
  m.accountnum.value = f.accountnum.value;

  // load another page in this frame
  window.location = "confirm.html";
}
```

Add validation routines to check that the user has made valid entries.

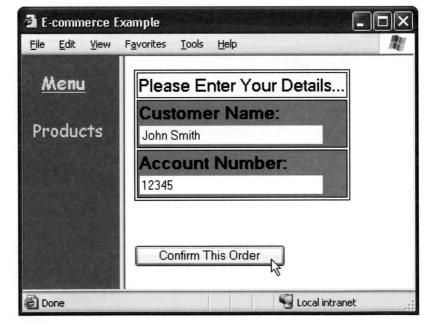

Generate an order number

The final page that appears in the order process contains all details of the customer's order for the user to confirm before submitting the order form.

These details are dynamically written by JavaScript with data retrieved from the hidden form **m** in the **menu** frame page.

It is useful to allocate a unique number to the customer's order for identification purposes.

The JavaScript on the confirmation page first generates this number, then stores it in the hidden form **m** in the **menu** frame.

Typically a **Date** object can provide an order number using parts of the current time concatenated into a single number.

In this script the order number will comprise the final number in the year followed by the month number, then the hour, minute and second:

*confirm.js
(part of)*

It is unlikely but possible that two different customers could generate the same order number at exactly the same time.

```
// variables for the form objects
var m = parent.frames.menu.document.forms.m;
var f = document.forms.f;

// generate a time-derived order number
var d = new Date();
var yr = ( d.getYear() ).toString();
yr = yr.charAt(3);
var mo = ( d.getMonth() ).toString();
var hr = ( d.getHours() ).toString();
var mn = ( d.getMinutes() ).toString();
var sc = (d.getSeconds() ).toString();
var onum = yr + mo + hr + mn + sc;

// store the order number with the other order data
m.ordernum.value = onum;
```

The script continues on the next page to dynamically write page content using data from the hidden form **m** to state the order number, customer name and account number.

Items required on the order and their quantity are then listed only for those items where the user has made an entry.

Confirm the order

*confirm.js
(cont'd)*

```
// write out the generated order number
document.write("Order No. " + m.ordernum.value);

// write out the customer details
document.write("<br/>For " + m.customer.value);
document.write("<br/>Account No." + m.accountnum.value);

// write out any ordered products
document.write("<hr/>");
if(m.ball.value != "")
document.write(m.ball.value+" Balls @ $7.99 each<br/>");
if(m.hoop.value != "")
document.write(m.hoop.value+" Hoops @ $3.99 each<br/>");
if(m.cone.value != "")
document.write(m.cone.value+" Cones @ $5.99 each<br/>");
```

Include this script in the body of the HTML document at the point where the details are to appear.

Add a feature to navigate back to the order page so the user can amend the order if required.

The **confirm.html** document contains a further hidden form with the **id** of **f** that exactly mirrors the hidden form **m** in the menu frame. When the user clicks the button on this page its **onclick** attribute calls a JavaScript function that copies all the values from form **m** to form **f**, then it submits form **f** to the server.

Submit the order

confirm.js (cont'd)

```
// a function to copy values from a hidden form in
// another frame into a local hidden form
// - then submit the local form to the server
function send_order()
{
    // copy the values from form m to form f
    f.customer.value = m.customer.value;
    f.accountnum.value = m.accountnum.value;
    f.ordernum.value = m.ordernum.value;
    f.ball.value = m.ball.value;
    f.hoop.value = m.hoop.value;
    f.cone.value = m.cone.value;

    // submit form f to the server
    f.submit();
}
```

In this example the **action** attribute of the **<form>** element specifies that this form data should be processed by a CGI script called **parser.cgi**. This server-side script simply sends a HTML Web page back to the browser listing all the form data keys and values that it has received.

*This routine could simply have submitted the hidden form **m** in the menu frame – but the response from the server would then have appeared in that frame.*

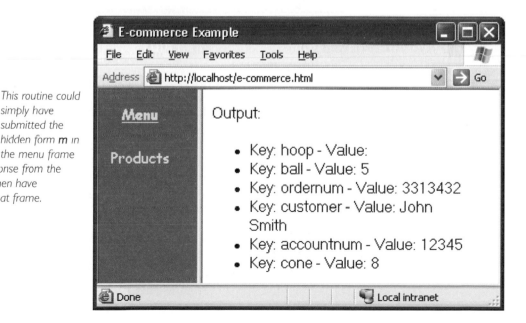

What next ?

The future looks bright for JavaScript with the introduction of the SVG file format to display Scalable Vector Graphics.

This file format stores vector graphic information in text form within a XML document.

File sizes of SVG images are very small compared to GIF and JPG images and have the advantage that the image can be scaled-up without increasing file size.

Also most importantly the elements of the image can be manipulated by JavaScript to create animation and interactive effects.

This illustration showing the text, star shape and drop-shadow effect is written in a text file using the SVG file format.

Learn more about the SVG file format from the W3C website at http://www.w3c.org.

Jasc Software, creators of Paint Shop Pro, have a program called WebDraw that creates vector graphics as SVG images available from their website at **http://www.jasc.com**.

Modern versions of Adobe Illustrator support SVG and include an Interactivity Palette to create dynamic SVG with JavaScript.

Adobe have also created the PC browser plug-in needed to support the SVG format which can be automatically installed on browsers without SVG capability and is freely available at **http://www.adobe. com/svg/viewer/install/**.

The further extension of the browser DOM together with these exciting developments in SVG should ensure that JavaScript will continue adding magic to future websites.

Index

O

N

P